POLITICAL RISK ASSESSMENT

Recent Titles in
Bibliographies and Indexes in Law and Political Science

Scottish Nationalism and Cultural Identity in the Twentieth Century: An Annotated Bibliography of Seconday Sources
Compiled by Gordon Bryan

Edwin S. Corwin and the American Constitution: A Bibliographical Analysis
Kenneth D. Crews

POLITICAL RISK ASSESSMENT
An Annotated Bibliography

Compiled by
DAVID A. JODICE

Bibliographies and Indexes in Law and Political Science, Number 3

Greenwood Press
Westport, Connecticut • London, England

Library of Congress Cataloging in Publication Data

Jodice, David A.
Political risk assessment.

(Bibliographies and indexes in law and political science, ISSN 0742-6909 ; no. 3)
Includes index.
1. Investments, Foreign—Political aspects—Bibliography. 2. Risk management—Political aspects—Bibliography. 3. Political stability—Evaluation—Bibliography. I. Title. II. Series.
Z7164.E17J63 1985 [HG4538] 016.6581'52 84-19784
ISBN 0-313-24444-8 (lib. bdg.)

Library of Congress Catalog Card Number: 84-19784
ISBN: 0-313-24444-8
ISSN: 0742-6909

First published in 1985

Greenwood Press
A division of Congressional Information Service, Inc.
88 Post Road West, Westport, Connecticut 06881

Printed in the United States of America

10 9 8 7 6 5 4 3 2 1

Contents

Acknowledgments

This review was the product, in part, of research conducted over several years on expropriation of foreign direct investment in natural resource extraction. Much of this work was carried out at the Center for International Affairs, Harvard University, and at the Science Center Berlin. I benefitted throughout from the ideas, encouragement and careful criticisms of Karl W. Deutsch, Stephen J. Kobrin, Charles L. Taylor, John S. Odell, Jorge I. Dominguez and many other colleagues at Harvard's Department of Government.

This annotated bibliography builds on analytic work done during the late 1970s. More recently, I have benefitted from the comments and questions of my students at Georgetown University. The course on political risk provided numerous opportunities to discuss the literature and new techniques in country risk assessment. Theodore H. Moran of Georgetown and Fariborz Ghadar of George Washington University have made valuable criticisms. I appreciate their support. The staff of Georgetown's Lauinger Library have been helpful throughout the preparation of this book.

During the preparation of this reference I have received invaluable programming support from Debra Dugger. I am grateful to James Sabin of Greenwood Press for his efficient and effective management of the production of the book. I alone am responsible for any errors of commission or omission.

D.A.J.
Washington, D.C.
June 1984

Introduction

The political risk profession is both new and rapidly growing. Expanding corporate interest in assessing foreign political environments is indicated, in part, through formal surveys (Kobrin, 1982) and the growth of a literature analyzing corporate practices. The Association of Political Risk Analysts was formed in 1980 and has a corporate and individual membership of approximately four hundred.

The literature of political risk is diverse in terms of subject matter and quality. This review will present an overview chapter on the field and annotated listings of recent publications (approximately 1970–1983) organized into thematic chapters. References are grouped into a chapter on multinational corporations in world politics (Chapter Two), a review of sources of political risk (Chapter Three), a description of analytic approaches to risk assessment and risk management (Chapter Four), and a listing of reference materials that will be useful to the risk analyst (Chapter Five). An Index is provided. Given the size of the field, certain limiting choices had to be made on the scope of the study. The focus is on the experience of political risk overseas, e.g. nationalizations, and restrictions on operations, and how American and foreign-based multinational companies and financial institutions have responded to these changes. We will not look at multinational management, except as it related to political risk management, nor will we examine theories of economic development, international trade, or foreign investment. Political instability has an impact on risk, and where that linkage is explicitly treated, references will be presented. However, we will not review the voluminous literature on political instability. That has been ably done elsewhere (Zimmerman, 1982). The substantial literature on economic forecasting is also not reviewed.

This reference builds on previous efforts to catalogue and review the literature on political risk. We have avoided, where possible, unnecessary duplication of previous bibliographies (Burtis, et.al., 1971). Edited collections and conference volumes are reported only once and under the name of the general editor. If mentioned in the annotation, individual authors and topics are included in the Index.

Much of the political risk literature in the trade and academic journals is concentrated in a few periodicals. Principal among these are the *Columbia Journal of World Business, Harvard Business Review*, and the *Journal of International Business Studies*. The academic journals that include articles related to political risk include *World Politics, International Organization, International Studies Quarterly, Journal of the Developing Areas, Economic Development and Cultural Change, The Journal of Inter- American Affairs, Comparative Politics*, and *Comparative Political Studies*. An additional important source is the official publication of the Association of Political Risk Analysts: *Political Risk Review*. This review publishes association and membership news, country-specific risk assessments, pieces on methods for analyzing risk, book notices, and a survey of salaries begun on an annual basis in 1982. The key legal journals are the *American Journal of International Law, Virginia Journal of International Law*, and the *Journal of World Trade Law*.

One aspect of the growth of the political risk profession is the selection and testing of analytic tools and methodologies. The best guide we have to what will work well in the future is what has been found useful in the recent past. Tools, databases and approaches that have demonstrated their utility (accuracy, timeliness, efficiency) will be accepted if the human and financial resources that are necessary for their effective use are made available. Multinational corporations and banks that are directly exposed to political risk will choose between alternative methods of shaping political risk estimates and incorporating the results of those estimates into the decision-making process.

Private sector consumers of political risk information face several choices: internal versus external development of political risk judgments, macro- versus micro-level assessment, and the choice of quantitative versus qualitative techniques. If the firm chooses to rely heavily on external sources of information, the choice between acquiring information streams or finished analytic judgments will still have to be made.

Consumers of political risk assessment will trust judgments only to the extent that they are derived from primary data that have been shown in the past to be related to political risk. Much has been made in the literature of the importance of political instability. Less has been done, however, to systematically track its relationship to changes in the operating environment for foreign business. Similarly, risk consultants have been remiss in not testing their own track records. Although one might debate the adequacy of such a standard, risk forecasters should be willing to publicly accept the same kind of testing that opinion pollsters receive at election time or the meteorologists face every day. Without a publicly verified track record, a consumer knows nothing about the validity or reliability of purported indicators of political risk.

This volume reviews analytic works and methodologies appropriate for the assessment and forecasting of political risk. It will serve as a guide to the field for corporate decisionmakers and managers of country/political risk assessment teams. Students of the environmental assessment practices of U.S.-based firms will find this a convenient introduction to the field. Analysts and managers in the international affairs agencies of the U.S. Government will turn to these references and their authors as they struggle to incorporate techniques from private industry into governmental assessment of foreign political developments.

The field of political risk assessment and management is new and evolving. The literature reported here describe the evolution of this field during the 1970s and early 1980s, and the development and testing of analytic approaches. At best, this volume is a one-time snapshot of a process that is moving, hopefully, in the direction of greater reliability and relevance to corporate needs.

POLITICAL RISK ASSESSMENT

Chapter One: An Overview of Political Risk Assessment

Political risk assessment has existed as a function since the development of the nation-state. Evaluating foreign political, economic and social conditions has long been a function of national governments and professional roles have developed to meet these functions. The functions that a diplomat or spy perform (observing, reporting, representing) are crucial to the thousands of American companies that have substantial overseas operations. Whether a firm has invested in a foreign country or is engaging in trade, it needs information on the likely future condition of the country and the policies that will affect its operating ability. While judgments about economic trends and social developments are important, we focus here on political risk because that is the area historically least regarded by American multinationals. Only recently has this function begun to evolve into a corporate role, posing organizational, resource and management questions for American companies (Root, 1968; Kobrin, 1982). The growing concern with the analysis and management of political risk assessment is evidenced by the growth of the profession (i.e., the Association of Political Risk Analysts) and recent empirical studies on the structuring of risk assessment in leading companies. This concern with organization, resources and management is appropriate. However, it is unfortunate that the profession has moved on to these issues before the prior analytic questions have been satisfactorily resolved.

Political risk assessment has developed largely in response to trends and developments external to multinational business. Aside from a basic precondition, i.e., the post-World War II international expansion of American business throughout the world by means of trade and investment, both the demand for risk assessment and the supply of potential risk analysts are exogenous to the firm. Demand has been driven by the increased perception (based on real experience) of greater risk in foreign operations derived directly from war, revolution, and civil violence or indirectly through government policy change (expropriation or nationalization of ownership; regulation of behavior; restrictions on sourcing or remission of earnings). Instances of nationalization have increased substantially since 1945 while the increasing sophistication of many Third World governments has whetted the regulatory knife.

The first major crack in the international regime for private foreign investment appeared with the Russian Revolution of 1917 where foreign investment was nationalized along with that of domestic entrepreneurs. That situation was seen as atypical -- the preserve of diplomats and lawyers -- and for many years that perception was correct. With the exception of a few isolated instances in the natural resource sector (Mexico in 1938, Iran in 1951, and Bolivia in 1952) nationalization of foreign investment was limited to a few countries undergoing revolutionary transformations (China, Eastern Europe, Egypt).

With the end of the major colonial empires in 1960, came a surge in national assertiveness toward the foreign investor. Formal independence, growing ties among Third World states, the formation of commodity cartels, activism in and by the United Nations, all served to increase the awareness on the part of host countries of the effects of foreign investors on their national development and, in many cases, provided the information and solidarity needed to do something about that dependence. These efforts to assert national control over economic life were accelerated in the early 1970s by the increasing influence of OPEC. Cresting in the 1973–74 oil embargo, OPEC's development as a cartel shifted bargaining power in the direction of the oil-producing countries. OPEC stimulated demands in the areas of production, pricing, taxation and royalties, and eventually, ownership. Continuing tensions and instability in the Third World (notably the Iranian Revolution) sharpened corporate interest in techniques useful for the assessment of political trends and policy changes.

On the supply side, political risk assessment was buttressed by the growth of social science in American universities, foundations and research institutes throughout the 1960s and 1970s. Behavioral social science reared a generation of scholars (potential analysts) trained in the application of data, statistical methodology and computer technology to the study of individuals, organizations, and nation-states. The development of behavioral science coincided with technological improvements in computer facilities (both hardware and software), federal funding and the expansion of American higher education to produce a bumper crop of well-trained political, social and economic analysts. It is out of this university environment that many of the most promising risk assessment techniques have emerged.

What is Political Risk?

Over the past several years many definitions have been offered for political risk. Political risk may be defined as:

> Changes in the operating conditions of foreign enterprises that arise out of the political process, either directly through war, insurrection, or political violence, or through changes in government policies that affect the ownership and behavior of the firm. Political risk can be conceptualized as events, or a series of events, in the national and international environments that can affect the physical assets, personnel, and operations of foreign firms.

Political risk is distinguished from the customary economic risks of business (marketing, competition, availability of inputs) including macroeconomic trends that affect business performance; and risks arising out of social changes (labor unionism, feminism, race relations) that are not an output of the political system. Of course, at the margin, these putative economic and social factors may be political products (i.e., laws governing collective bargaining) and at that point the distinctiveness of political risk disappears. The interrelationship of these factors has inclined practitioners to speak of country risk. Either way, one has to look at the political process in order to shape judgments about the likelihood of nationalization or expropriation or changing administrative behavior.

International Law and Political Risk

International lawyers have been interested in the relevance of the norms of international law for the identification and resolution of particular investment disputes. Therefore, their contributions deal largely with the legal validity of a given nationalization. Under this rubric, they evaluate the legality of a measure, assess the role of foreign courts, discuss investment protection policies by both public and private actors, and analyse the results of the *post facto* bargaining process. Legal scholars are concerned not with the causes of risk, but with its consequences for the continued operation of the firm, bilateral relations with the home country, and the payment of compensation. Frequently in the published research, political or economic nationalism is assumed as the cause of expropriation while attention is focused on the results.

There are four criteria by which the legal validity of expropriations is evaluated. These are (1) that expropriation is a formal action of state sovereignty; (2) that the property be taken in the public interest; (3) that the action be non-discriminatory with regard to targets; and (4) that "prompt, adequate, and effective compensation" be paid to the injured parties. An act of expropriation is valid under international law if it is undertaken by a sovereign state with appropriate enabling legislation. The state in this usage refers to national, regional, or local governments, as well as all agencies of those bodies. Although a few expropriations were initiated at the sub-national level -- with the public utilities expropriations in the Brazilian state of Rio Grande do Sul in 1962 receiving much attention -- most acts are undertaken by national governments. Such acts of state are valid only if they are applied in a manner consistent with enabling legislation. This last point is not undisputed, however. White has argued that an expropriation is valid regardless of its constitutional origin. The other criteria of validity are more important than the source of authority for such action. (White, 1961, p.41)

The requirement that property be taken in the public interest, and that it be returned when the purpose to which it is put has changed, places strict bounds on the legitimacy of a given nationalization under international law. Explanations which are acceptable under international law are labor disputes, dissatisfaction with the performance of foreign firms (including the possibility that the enterprise is going to suspend operations), the vacancy or abandonment of property by its owners (this occurred in Algeria, Angola, and Mozambique after independence), and the elastic argument that the state be allowed to "put under its protection property whose method of acquisition, operation or utilization could disturb law and order or social peace." (*Le Monde*, May 17, 1963, p. 9). While the preservation of law and order are certainly public purposes, the wording of the above text and the manner in which it was applied in Algeria in the early 1960s, leave some doubt about the validity of those nationalizations under international law. It also illustrates the plasticity of these requirements in the face of domestic pressures for nationalization.

The determination of the validity of the public purpose is not always so ambiguous. A case in point is the Libyan expropriation of British Petroleum in December 1971. The official explanation was that the British Petroleum Exploratory Company (Libya), Ltd., was taken in retaliation for Britain's failure to prevent Iran from seizing some islands in the Persian Gulf. The Libyan representative at the United Nations Security Council argued that the policy change was motivated by the political objective of hurting the interests of Great Britain.

The third validity criterion is that the taking be non-discriminatory. The Libyan expropriation was clearly in violation of this principle. For a given act of state to satisfy the non-discrimination requirement, all firms in a given sector (domestic and foreign-owned) would have to be nationalized. There are two problems, however, with this interpretation of the non-discrimination principle. First, following the ruling of the Bremen Court of Appeals with regard to the taking of Dutch property in Indonesia, Domke has argued that "the equality concept means only that equals must be treated equally and that the different treatment of unequals is admissible." Second, if the industry is totally owned by foreign firms, e.g., gasoline distribution in Sri Lanka in the early 1960s, then the nationalization of these enterprises cannot by definition be discriminatory.

The fourth validity criteria is that "prompt, adequate, and effective compensation" be paid to the injured party. But, what does this actually mean in practice? With reference to U.S. policy (e.g., the Hickenlooper Amendment) prompt means that serious negotiations for compensation will be undertaken within six months of the nationalization. Of course, the problem of distinguishing substantive negotiations undertaken in good faith from window dressing on the part of the expropriating government or the U.S. Department of State remains. The adequacy of compensation is also difficult, if not impossible, to assess. Does compensation refer to the book value of the property? If so, at what point in time? Inflation and changes in equity position will cause the book value of the subsidiary at the time of entry into the host economy to bear little or no relation to its market value or worth to the parent corporation at the time of taking. Although one could argue that adequate compensation would be the free market price of a given firm as a going concern, it is impossible to determine the market price for an affiliate of a vertically-integrated multinational company that is facing imminent state takeover. What is an effective medium of payment? It should be in a currency that will be of immediate economic use to the recipient. Such hard currencies will be in short supply in most less developed countries, however, and there is a tendency to pay compensation in the national currency or government bonds. An example of this problem is the nationalization of the American Life Insurance Company by the government of Pakistan on March 19, 1972. At that time a settlement was agreed to by both parties with payment to be made in rupees. By the time of payment in September of that year, the rupee had depreciated by 130 percent and the company claimed that it had not received adequate compensation.

One additional general problem remains with regard to compensation for nationalized property. A number of Third World spokesmen have argued that no compensation is due the multinationals because of the "excess profits" that they have systematically extracted from the LDCs. This approach by numerous nationalizing governments threatens the basis of international legal norms governing the treatment of foreign investment.

Analytic Approaches to Economic Nationalism

The initial response to economic nationalism (the old name for political risk) was largely diplomatic. Only when economic nationalism coincided with the threat of communist expansion did the Western powers intervene militarily. These interventions (Russia, Iran, Egypt) had mixed results that overall discouraged the use of force in investment disputes (Krasner, 1978). During the interwar and much of the postwar periods economic nationalism was seen as a problem of enforcing international law (e.g., the Mexican oil nationalizations of 1938, Eastern Europe after 1945) through diplomatic means. In these instances attention was centered on the payment of compensation -- insuring that it was prompt, adequate and effective -- rather than disputing the right of sovereign states to nationalize private property for a public purpose. Much of the early literature on expropriation focused on these legal questions, often castigating nationalizing governments as politically immature and economically naive, rather than probing the causes of economic nationalism.

As instances of political risk began to multiply during the 1960s and 1970s, the topic acquired importance for scholars interested in the economics of development, political development and modernization, and comparative approaches to developing countries in general. Consistent with the methodological thrust of comparative politics, most of these early studies were in a case study format. Scholars focused on single countries, often Third World natural resource exporters (Moran, 1974; Tugwell, 1975). Gradually, more genuinely comparative studies emerged. These chronicled nationalizations by several countries in a specific region (Ingram, 1974) or, as was more often the case, were industry studies (Jacoby, 1974).

Expropriation as a "Psychic Commodity"

After the international lawyers have examined the legal implications of an expropriation dispute, the problem of causal explanation remains. The "pyschic commodity" approach has received widespread attention in the literature on nationalization. After demonstrating that Third World nations consider some industries "strategic" (that different sectors are strategic at different levels of modernization) to their plans for economic development, and that there is a general preference in the developing countries for public as opposed to private enterprise. Harry Johnson (1965) devised a theory of economic nationalism. He argued that governing elites, and the population at large from which they derive a measure of support or at least passive and habitual obedience, are often willing to sacrifice material advantages for the psychic satisfaction of seeing foreigners displaced by nationals in high prestige roles. Drawing on the work of Gary S. Becker, Johnson has substituted "for a taste for discrimination a taste for nationalism."

Following Anthony Downs, Johnson has integrated a political element into his model of economic nationalism. Arguing that both leaders and followers in politics have limited time and will act rationally in the allocation of that time to political action, Johnson has proposed that economic nationalism can be a vital element in the communications flow between political elites and the population. The development of symbols of national identity and purpose can ease the difficulties of communicating across large numbers of diverse people and serve to build a sense of identity with the nation and those state institutions which have acted vigorously against the foreigner. A political party in a democracy exchanges policies for votes on election day. In a competitive political system, parties need to communicate their policy preferences to the electorate as economically as possible. One way of doing this will be to focus on the problems for national development and autonomy posed by a large foreign presence in the local economy. Thus, political parties can use expropriation to attain office or maintain themselves in power. Few of the world's new nations are democracies, however. How applicable is this framework to authoritarian political systems?

> Nationalistic feeling provides a foundation for the establishment of a preclusive ideology as a pre-requisite

> for one-party government; and there is evident connection between the stridency of nationalism in the new nations and their propensity to establish one-party governments. Even where the two-party system is maintained, the competition in ideology would tend to make both parties stress nationalism and nationalistic policies if there were widespread nationalistic sentiment among the electorate (Johnson, 1965, p.175).

As the above arguments have shown, we cannot go much further without defining nationalism. Following Webster, nationalism is "a sense of national consciousness exalting one nation above all others and placing primary emphasis on the promotion of its culture and interests as opposed to those of other nations or supranational groups." Nationalism is a sentiment among a population that guides the decision processes of its members with regard to international and intranational policy choices. Nationalism is the propensity of a group to make decisions in favor of its own nationality. As Karl Deutsch has argued in *Nationalism and Social Communication:*

> A nationality is a people pressing to acquire a measure of effective control over the behavior of its members. It is a people striving to equip itself, with some machinery of compulsion strong enough to make the enforcement of its commands sufficiently probably to aid in the spread of habits of voluntary compliance with them.

The sense of identity as a nation intensifies into nationalism as the country undergoes the experience of modernization. The systematic preference for one's own nation and the individuals or organizations that constitute it over those from other nations is a necessary and definitive sign of nationalism. The point to be remembered here is that this pattern of preferences is systematically apparent and theoretically measurable throughout the population under consideration.

Nationalism is important to the understanding of expropriation for a number of reasons. The preference for national instead of foreign actors in the minds of the decision makers and their domestic audiences will serve as a guide, conscious or otherwise, for policy selection. It is one of the motive forces behind the pressure for local control of key sectors of the economy. Furthermore, the principle of nationalism itself will provide convenient rationalization for a politics of expropriation. This rationalization will find many receptive ears within a given nation as well as in international organizations. Daniel Blanchard argued in *The Journal of International Law and Economics* that nationalism is a necessary part of the study of political risk because it "...provides an explanation for a multitude of past failures by laying the blame on foreign domination and exploitation, and at the same time promises a brighter future through increased national power."

The desire to be free from dependence on foreign sources of economic wealth and political power animates in large measure the behavior of governing elites. In Latin America, President Eduardo Frei enunciated his program of "Chileanization" in a May 21, 1969 speech to the Congress.

> ...The determination of the government to obtain a larger participation in the higher prices of copper satisfies a just national aspiration and incorporates into our copper policy the new factor that the copper market is now indicating by stable trends. This determination will thus signify a higher benefit for the nation making new resources available in coming years.

Although nationalism is theoretically measurable with such instruments as content analysis or population surveys, the difficulties of conducting such research that would satisfy the requirements of cross-national validity and reliability for a large number of nations at one point in time are insurmountable. Even though the extent of nationalistic sentiment and the intensity with which national values are held would theoretically very from case to case according to the variables specified by Deutsch (level and rate of social mobilization, extent of ethnolinguistic diversity), we can consider nationalism to be a constant in terms of its effects on political choices of governing elites at the level of the nation-state. Nationalism is present in all the countries as a determinant of the parameters of political action, and even though we are unable to measure its effects directly, we must recognize its existence as a powerful causal factor in the process of political risk.

Johnson (1965) draws on the work of Albert Breton to characterize expropriations as investments in nationality.

> *Nationality*, then, is a form of capital which can be augmented through investment or reduced depreciation and consumption. *Nationalism* is both the disposition that leads an individual to favor and justify investment in nationality and the encouragement which he gives to the investment of present scarce resources for the alteration of the inter-ethnic or inter-national distribution of ownership.

Investment in nationality leads to two different types of benefits. First, and perhaps most important, there is the diffuse sense of satisfaction following the transfer of resources from foreign to national ownership. The new owner may be a private citizen or corporation, or the state itself. If the former are recipients of shares in an expropriated firm at concessional terms or if nationals are given high positions previously the preserve of foreigners, then tangible and direct benefits will result from nationalization. Some of these benefits will remain even if the firm receives compensation for its assets. It should be noted, however, that nationalization will have important distributional implications that vary with the extent of compensation, the progressiveness of the tax system, future employment practices, and the extent to which nationals are able to acquire shares of the subsidiary at less than the "market price." Breton has argued that nationalization is less income producing than it is income distributing. Until we analyze more empirical data on the relationship between changes in the national regime for foreign investment and the distribution of income, we can only conclude that international, but not necessarily intra-national redistribution occurs with expropriation of foreign direct investment.

What hypotheses can we generate from this brief review? First, we conclude that certain sectors of the economy will be more vulnerable to expropriation because of their salience and importance to national security and economic development. Among these would be public utilities, resource extraction, and finance (banking and insurance). Second, because confiscation is a useful development tool, we would expect the rate of expropriation to vary with the level of modernization of the host country. Third, any model that will be useful in explaining expropriation will have a certain cross- national variance for which it cannot account. This "unexplained" variance is largely due to the role of ideology (nationalism, central planning, state corporatism) which instructs political elites in the selection of goals and the means by which they can be attained.

There are a number of problems with the economics of nationalism approach, however, that make it unsuitable or at least inadequate as a general approach to political risk. The basic basic deficiency is the specification of nationalism as the major explanatory variable. All states exhibit some forms of nationalism and we have no way of systematically assessing the relationship between the intensity of nationalistic sentiment and its distribution throughout segments of the population, and the policies that governments enact with regard to such firms. By explaining everything, nationalism explains nothing. Arguments from nationalism can be used to explain war, international prejudice, and internal conflict, as well as foreign economic policies that emphasize national welfare over global stability and efficiency. This argument tells us nothing about the timing and scale of expropriation in various sectors of the national economy. The economics of nationalism school presents a misleading analysis of expropriation because it neglects the individuals and groups through whom such calculations about economic development choices and foreign policy decisions are made: the governing political elites. The authors discussed above have both neglected the economic rationality of confiscation, and have understated the political rationality, from the perspective of elite power maintenance, of manipulating the foreign investor before domestic audiences.

The Appeal of Confiscation

An alternative to the psychic commodity approach is a model derived by Martin Bronfenbrenner (1953/54) to explain nationalization in terms of the concrete economic development benefits that it brings to the host country. He argued that confiscation can be a useful policy alternative for elites that want to increase the rate, or modify the course, of economic modernization. Noting the Soviet and Chinese examples, Bronfenbrenner observed that nationalization has not killed the goose that lays the golden eggs. Using a theoretical model based on a hypothetical case of a less-developed, over-populated country, Bronfenbrenner developed three models of foreign economic policy to demonstrate the benefits of confiscating assets that do not belong to nationals. The *laissez- faire* model results in stagnation. Real income fails to expand because of population growth. This is compared to the revolutionary (Soviet) model in which income from the maintenance of the now dispossessed classes (or foreign enterprises) is directed to the state's development program. The taking of the wealth of the upper classes in the great revolutions of the twentieth century is analogous to the nationalization of foreign-owned property by Third World states in a more recent period. A populist model has the disadvantages of the Soviet model (resource leakages into symbolic demonstrations, party and policy functionaries; large military establishments; inefficiencies in resource allocation; the slowing of innovation; and renewed population growth) while it also shifts income from savers to spenders, thereby slowing the rate of economic growth. As Bronfenbrenner has argued, the choice between these development models depends on the preferences of the governing elites, the level of development of the country in question, and the constraints that other actors in the international system can exert on national policymaking.

Having argued that confiscation makes sense from the perspective of the developing countries, Bronfenbrenner listed eight factors that make the world relatively unsafe for foreign capital in the last half of the twentieth century. He observed that the histories of Great Britain and the United States should be seen as exceptions, rather than as the norm for government/business interactions. These factors will be helpful in the development of a theory to explain the timing, extent and sectoral focus of expropriation. They are:

(1) Limited upward social mobility in the developing countries which will produce frustration among large numbers of the population.

(2) Nationalism directs political choices against foreigners and in favor of groups within the host country.

(3) The central planning and rapid development ethic fueled and aided in part by the developed countries themselves stimulates a bias toward statism among Third World governing elites.

(4) Conspicuous consumption and the investments of local elites as well as foreign firms will affect the structure of the national regime for foreign investment.

(5) Increased governmental capability in the twentieth century relative to the resources available to the modernizing monarchs of early modern Europe make direct state control of economic activity more viable.

(6) Informal confiscation was an aspect of western expansion (secularizing church properties, taking land and resources from the indigenous populations of the western hemisphere) and many of the developed states have public corporations in sectors vital to national security and welfare such as aerospace, electricity, and transportation.

(7) The decline in the deference shown to private property is having a powerful negative effect on the ability of foreign investors to justify their existence and protect their assets.

(8) The populations in the less developed nations are too highly mobilized and aware of the consumption patterns of the national and international elites to willingly reduce their own meager consumption in the interests of a development program with high short-run costs and deferred benefits. Justifiably,

> they want to see concrete improvements in their condition now.

This listing of various national and international variables that are relevant to expropriation will be useful in generating hypotheses to explain why governing elites alter longstanding behavioral patterns and nationalize or expropriate foreign firms. We can now go beyond the methodology used by Bronfenbrenner and test causal theories of expropriation with reliable data that are publicly available for most of the relevant Third World states. Although Bronfenbrenner's listing would generate hypotheses about the relationship between economic policy and such variables as the level of development, the rate of growth, the size distribution of income, the demonstration effects of other host countries' policies toward foreign direct investment, and the ability of the major powers to enforce international property norms, we need a systematic and comprehensive theory that will have general applicability, rather than relying on ad hoc or *sui generis* explanations of particular cases.

Social Science Approaches to Economic Nationalism

Social science approaches began to make an impact on the assessment of economic nationalism/political risk during the early 1970s (Truitt, 1974; Knudsen, 1974). The greater availability of data on nationalization itself and on host country attributes, prompted studies of broader scope (Kobrin, 1980; Jodice, 1980). These four studies are representative of a substantial number of works that attempted to derive general conclusions about the factors that cause political risk (most often measured as formal nationalization or expropriation) as evidenced in the best empirical data available.

Truitt's study was pathbreaking in two ways. First, working in a business context, he applied general comparative methods to the problem of nationalization. Second, he deduced an impressive number of hypotheses about political risk that, although not all were adequately tested in his own work, have served as a rich mine for subsequent analysts.

Truitt did his comparative work at two levels: the nationalized subsidiary and the host country. Data were gathered on the attributes of 54 nationalized affiliates of British and American companies in 11 developing countries between 1945 and 1969. These data showed that size, sector, foreign exchange activities, localization of management, public relations skills, and the extent of the firm's strategic vulnerability to the loss of the local subsidiary were important factors affecting vulnerability to political risk. Nationality of the parent firm and ownership structure had little effect on the vulnerability to nationalization.

Data on the attributes of nationalizing countries were also collected. Cross–tabulations of these national attributes with propensity to expropriate indicated that modernity (GNP per capita), the public sector -- private sector mix, political (in)stability, the colonial heritage, and the extent of indigenous entrepreneurial talent affect the propensity to expropriate. The ideology of the ruling elite, the country's standing in international law and the condition of its balance of payments were unrelated to its level of activity against foreign investors.

Knudsen's work differed from Truitt's in regional focus and the use of more elaborate statistical tools (factor analysis, multiple regression, discriminant analysis). Knudsen followed Truitt in examining both firms and countries in order to evaluate the conditions that determine country risk and the vulnerability of classes of firms or specific industries.

Knudsen's work focused on the treatment of foreign investment in 21 Latin American countries from 1968–1971. In an important departure from Truitt's practice, Knudsen included both expropriators and non-expropriators. This allows for the detection of the presence and strength of a cause (e.g., high repatriation of profits) in expropriating countries and a search for it in non- expropriating countries. Our confidence in the value of an indicator is enhanced if it is present (or of greater value) in an expropriating country and absent (or of lesser value) in a non-expropriating country. Without this larger frame of reference, we can have little confidence in statements about the attributes of politically risky countries.

At the level of the firm, Knudsen found that size and sector were the most important factors affecting likelihood of expropriation. At the national level, system stability, differences between expectations and welfare at the mass level, the abundance of natural resources, the organization of labor and the extent of political modernization all effected political risk. Measured at the national level, the scale and sectoral concentration of foreign direct investment had a strong correlation with expropriation.

The strength of Knudsen's findings is indicated, in part, by the power of his discriminant analysis. The discriminant function for country risk correctly allocated 20 of 21 countries into a High-, Medium-, or Low- risk category. Of course, this was an exercise in post-dicting. No actual, real-time forecasts were attempted.

Truitt's and Knudsen's work share some limitations that have been remedied in subsequent studies. Both severely under-represent the incidence of nationalization. Truitt reported on 54 takings of British and American firms for the period 1945–1969. The absence of data on other capital-exporting states, e.g., (Italy, Netherlands, Portugal, France) distorts the findings. Knudsen reports 35 firms nationalized in Latin America between 1968 and 1971, substantially fewer than actually occurred. A second, and perhaps more severe limitation, is the failure to disaggregate the cross-national analysis by economic sector. Different economic and political factors effect the propensity to expropriate across different sectors of the economy: agriculture, petroleum production, mining and smelting, manufacturing, public utilities, transportation and communication, and trade. Lumping these sectors together into one national measure obscures important differences in causation, confounding accurate measurement and analysis. Knudsen's work on firm characteristics was limited to subsidiaries in high expropriation countries. This biases his findings. Firms in countries like Chile were caught up in a general socialization of the economy which is different from being singled out for discriminatory expropriations based on firm- specific characteristics.

More recent analyses (Kobrin, 1980; Jodice, 1980) benefitted from an exhaustive cross-national dataset on expropriation collected on behalf of the United Nations Centre on Transnational Corporations. This dataset covers all developing countries (including 80 expropriators) from 1960–79 and reports 588 separate nationalizations involving 1,958 foreign subsidiaries from approximately 15 capital-exporting states. Coded from public documents, this dataset is comprehensive with respect to country of incorporation, nationality of parent firm and economic sector. It is an essential tool for looking at political risk from the perspective of the host country. The database covers all developing countries and represents the sum of coercive actions taken against all foreign investors, regardless of their nationality.

Kobrin provides a basis for assessing attributes at the firm level conducive to expropriation. He compared nationalized firms with the general population of foreign subsidiaries according to such variables as: sector, size, parent nationality, and ownership structure. Kobrin found that political risk was greatest, during this period, for firms in resource extraction, public utilities and among manufacturing firms with mature and stable technologies. Risk was greater for firms that loomed large in the domestic economy and for joint ventures. Local partnerships with either the state or private entrepreneurs increased risk, primarily by increasing local knowledge about the technical and managerial aspects of the business.

Jodice's analysis focused on the resource extraction sector (petroleum production/mining and smelting) for the 50 developing countries that met the inclusion criteria of political independence as of 1967 and a 1967 stock of foreign direct investment in these sectors of at least U.S. $5 million. Aggregate level data were collected to test hypotheses about the effects on the propensity to expropriate of host country attributes, foreign investment characteristics, and host country dependence on the international system. Predictive data were collected for 1967 and regressed on an expropriation propensity score covering the years 1968–77.

The following host country attributes were related to political risk: modernity, government capacity, macroeconomic decay, and changes in the level of overt political violence directed against the government. Foreign investment attributes were measured at the national level to reflect the micro-level factors that Kobrin found to affect risk. These included the scale of foreign investment relative to GNP, the sectoral concentration of investment (the enclave economy), the concentration of investment by parent nationality, and the costs to the economy (measured by repatriation of earnings). National status in the international system is also related to the propensity to expropriate foreign firms. Weak and dependent countries are less likely to challenge the foreign investor. Country size, trade dependence (commodity concentration and export partner concentration) and foreign aid dependence exerted substantial negative effects on the propensity to expropriate.

Political risk assessment as an analytic endeavor has come a long way from early efforts in the diplomatic and legal arenas. The infusion of social science techniques (hypothesis testing, data collection, comparative analysis) into risk assessment has taken us far down the road of identifying empirically verified indicators that will build toward a tracking system. Two levels of analysis are necessary for an understanding of the dynamics of political risk. One needs to look at the larger national environment as well as the attributes of specific firms or projects in order to assess political risk.

What Political Risk Analysts Should Be Watching

The quantitative literature as well as country or industry studies have marked out five areas that the political risk analyst should watch.

(1) Impetus toward national control over the economy.

(2) Performance of the macroeconomy.

(3) Political stability in the host country.

(4) International autonomy/dependence of the host country.

(5) Obsolescing of bargains between the host government and foreign firms.

National control over key economic sectors has received much attention in recent years. The converse of global interdependence is the loss, or perception of loss, of national control over the economic actors and trends that affect welfare and security. The political risk literature of the 1970s and 1980s, unlike that of the previous two decades, treats national control as a valid and understandable requirement for policymaking at the national level. The early literature saw national control as a psychic commodity -- an indicator of political immaturity. Longstanding West European and Japanese concerns about American economic dominance, and American reactions to inward foreign direct investment, put Third World concerns about foreign control in perspective. Business firms have come to expect policy activism on the part of Third World governments. The point now is not to disparage change, but to anticipate it and guard against its negative effects.

Performance of the national economy is another cluster of variables that can cause political risk. When times are hard, governing elites are under pressure to find instrumental solutions to national problems. Because of their large role in national economic life and their impact on external flows, foreign investors will receive more than their share of attention during periods of economic stress. Levels of employment and production, exports and foreign exchange balances are going to be the target of host government scrutiny during the lean times. During the good times, foreign firms are less likely to be targeted for action but still may be subject to governmental intervention in the areas of social policy, indigenization of management, technology transfer and spin-off effects. Performance of the national economy is important also because it effects the stability of the political system and the durability of the government. Measures of national performance include GNP growth (in real and per capita terms), industrialization, inflation, full employment, ability to service external debt, and stable and growing earnings from exports.

Political instability is the most frequently cited factor among political risk watchers. Without being very sure what is meant by the term, political instability is touted universally as a major source of risk for foreign investors. In its direct effects, instability can cause loss or harm to a multinational through damage to its property, injury or death of its personnel, or loss of sales through disruption or intimidation. Less directly, political instability can influence government policy. A wide variety of scholars including Samuel P. Huntington and Ted Robert Gurr, have pointed out the relationship between threats to the power of the governing elite and the likelihood of actions against the foreign firm. Taking action against foreign investors can serve instrumental purposes (e.g., stopping the outflow of capital) and symbolic purposes (national integration, rally round the flag, etc.). A number of authors have found empirical evidence to support the hypothesis that governments under political pressure are more likely to nationalize foreign direct investment, *ceteris paribus*, than are governments that are not facing such challenges. (Truitt, 1974; Knudsen, 1974; Jodice, 1980).

Measures of the potential for political instability can also aid the risk analyst by tracking the probability of social revolution. Such basic transformations of the socioeconomic and political systems of developing countries have caused 40 percent of the 588 takings during the period 1960–79. Although the selective taking may be more common, the impact of large-scale, multi-sector nationalizations in Cuba, Peru, Chile, Egypt, Libya, Angola, Mozambique, Iran, and elsewhere has been substantial. While the political risk effects of national independence are largely a spent asset, there is no evidence to support the notion that major revolutions in the developing areas are obsolete.

Indicators of political instability can be developed from data presented in the third *World Handbook of Political and Social Indicators* (Taylor and Jodice, 1983). These daily event indicators of political protest, rebellion, government change and coercion can be aggregated to suit the analyst's needs allowing comparisons across time and countries. These unique political violence data are available in a current mode and are already in computer-readable form.

The international status of the host country is an indicator of the likelihood of political risk. Small, dependent countries are less likely to antagonize the foreign investor, the parent government and international organizations. This generalization is not a law, as the case of Cuba indicates. However, the Cuban case illuminates rather than invalidates the rule. Although Cuba was highly dependent on the United States, its leaders perceived an alternative in economic and political relations with the Soviet Union and Eastern Europe. To the extent that small countries can play off the multinationals and Western countries among each other, or receive support from international institutions and Third World organizations, their scope for action is expanded. The trend is towards more alternatives for governments that host foreign direct investment. Measures of host country status include size (not likely to change in the short- term), foreign aid dependence, concentration of export commodities and export-receiving countries, and financial ties to key foreign countries.

The obsolescing bargain model has become the dominant paradigm in the literature on political risk. It focuses on changes in the bargaining positions of governments and firms as the latter evolve from entry to termination. Over time bargaining strength has swung in the direction of Third World governments. But, these movements have been uneven and vary from sector to sector. This model has been especially useful in explaining nationalizations in natural resource extraction. The bargaining model directs attention to key variables, expanding its applicability beyond the natural resource sectors. These variables are: maturity and stability of the technology, extent to which capital is sunk at the outset or is invested incrementally across time, competitiveness of international markets for exported products, location of key bottlenecks in a (vertically-integrated) industry, and the level of information available to the host government about the industry and specific firms and projects. In effect, if the multinational manager places himself in the position of the host government he can evaluate the costs and benefits of action against specific foreign firms. This rational calculus should be supplemented with informed judgments about non-economic factors that may bias or overcome economic assessments (nationalism, political instability, ideology).

The obsolescing bargain model explains the dynamics and timing of disputes in the natural resource extraction sector of foreign direct investment. This model posits a relationship between two parties, in this case the state and a multinational corporation, which is intrinsically unstable because of their changing relative strengths over time. The initial bargain resulted in very few benefits for the host country and offered a large scope for unhindered and very profitable operations by foreign firms. As a cumulative long-run shift in bargaining power occurs, political elites in the host country will seek to restructure the agreement in the face of domestic political pressures and positive policy objectives.

What are the sources of bargaining strength? Minimally, one could rank the participants in the bargaining process along such dimensions as information, uncertainty, organizational capabilities and available financial resources. Before a large lump-sum investment in resource extraction is made, the position of the firm is very strong. Uncertainty dominates the situation. Neither the firm nor the government is aware of the availability of resources in the country and the state is willing to offer very favorable terms in what for it is a no-lose situation. Over time, however, as capital is irrevocably invested and resources are discovered, the original bargain appears too permissive to national political figures. Pressures build in the political system for revision of the original agreement as nationals become aware of the world market for the product in question and of their low relative share in the benefits of its production. This model is especially appropriate for the analysis of expropriation of natural resource firms because these are characterized by large, sunk investments and high political sensitivity. Dissatisfaction often results because the benefits of foreign participation in national development come early (employment, resource exploitation, capital inflows) while the costs are apparent after a time lag (profit repatriation, interference in domestic politics, linkages to great power politics).

In order to expand the analysis beyond resource firms, Moran has suggested three dimensions which can explain the likelihood of conflict or cooperation between the host government and foreign enterprise. These dimensions demonstrate that:

(1) The target of host government policy will depend on the salience and political sensitivity of the industry or firm.

(2) The setting is the perception of the contribution of the foreign firm to the economic growth and development of the host country. This dimension raises the question of the opportunity cost of political risk. How well can Venezuela, Chile, or Zambia, for example, progress without the participation of foreign enterprises in attaining the national goals of growth, modernization, etc., that are common to most Third World countries?

(3) The process of policy formation will vary with the degree to which social forces penetrate directly into the policymaking process. Do political elites bargain

> autonomously with the foreign firm? Does the governing regime bargain under intense pressure against its continuing rule? Or do various social and political groups participate directly in the bargaining process?

By using these dimensions for cataloging instances of expropriation, we can draw the distinctions between resource-producing firms and those that are active in other sectors of the host economy. A natural resource firm will have a high level of salience in a less developed country, at least in part because of its size, but also because of legal norms concerning the ownership and use of subsoil wealth. If a firm's size decreases (in absolute terms through declining sales or divestment; or in terms relative to national economic growth), then we would expect expropriation to occur because the retaliatory power of the firm had decreased.

Depending on the level of development, the ideology and administrative power of the state, and the degree of political instability in the host country, a foreign firm would be relatively secure. A manufacturing firm can be said to bring a high level of economic benefits (employment, technology transfer, and spin-offs in employee training), to be a symbol of economic and political modernity, and be innocuous to national political groups. If we look at the frequency of expropriation of manufacturing firms relative to that of resource firms, holding their relative shares of foreign direct investment constant, we can measure the degree to which host countries perceive certain firms and sectors as threats to vital national interests and ambitions.

The obsolescing bargain model is a significant improvement over earlier models of political risk. Its major advantage is that it encourages us to expect expropriation (or more subtle measures) as a natural aspect of economic and political modernization, and not as a pathology of underdeveloped polities. A few caveats are in order, however. First, we have the problem of heroic assumptions which underlay this application of game theory. The second objection is the failure of the model to incorporate third parties explicitly into the bargaining process. Third, the obsolescing bargain model assumes that the most significant variables are economic in nature. Explicitly, political pressures on host country elites to nationalize foreign firms are discounted or entirely overlooked.

With regard to the first problem, the obsolescing bargain model assumes at each stage of the negotiating process accurate and full information on the part of both parties. Are the payoffs really measurable and known? Can either predict what the actions and reactions of the other party will be? Tugwell faces this problem by introducing the idea of assertive experimentation where each party "muddles through" by feeling out the objectives and knowledge of its opponent. As the polity develops and political participation expands, the causal connections between various policies and the payoff matrix change. A certain level of taxation would have been considered more than adequate for Venezuelan petroleum in 1925. By 1950, a 25 percent tax rate was no longer enough, and would have resulted in negative political returns to the individuals or groups proposing it.

Second, and more important, the obsolescing bargain model abstracts from the international environment in which the negotiating occurs. Absent from the analysis is a systematic consideration of the behavior of other firms. Huntington has argued that the primary bargaining chip of the host state is control over access to its territory. As the number of competing multinationals expands, the value of this chip increases. In addition, one must consider the impact on the decisionmaking process of the threats of other extra-national actors. Among these actors we include the capital-exporting states, private commercial banks, the World Bank, and the International Monetary Fund.

There are political factors at work in the relationship between host governments and multinational enterprises. Host country elites do make calculations about the probable economic costs and benefits of foreign investment regime change to their country. The obsolescing bargain model overlooks the dilemmas of political impatience and pressure on governing elites to act against the multinational corporation in defense of its legitimacy and power. Under certain conditions of political stress, expropriation will occur even if it is not in the immediate or long-run interest of host country welfare.

Managing Risk Assessment

We began with the observation that most attention of the profession at this point is focused on the organization and management of political assessment within the firm. Although all the analytic issues have not been resolved, it is appropriate to worry the problem of managing risk assessment so that it makes an effective contribution to strategic planning, investment decision-making, and capital- budgeting.

The tasks of risk assessors fall into four categories:

(1) Identification of risk related factors.

(2) Prediction of government policy or risk factors arising directly out of the political process.

(3) Deciding effective corporate response.

(4) Executing the decisions (avoidance, exit, protective strategies).

We indicated above the factors that political risk analysts should be watching. Their ability to make probabilistic predictions will be evaluated in the next section on available risk assessment techniques. Whether political risk analysts should be involved in making corporate level decisions and executing same is a matter hotly debated in the literature and many corporate offices as well. The political risk analyst who avoids the decision- making process gains in objectivity but at the cost of influence. If the political analyst is offering information of value to decision- makers, he is likely to find that others in the organization will begin to use that information, thereby placing a barrier between analysis and decision-making. Over the long-term this will hurt the professional prospects of the political analyst without protecting him from the fallout of incorrect analytic judgments. The balancing act for the political analyst is between an objectivity that may lead to irrelevance and a participatory orientation that may place his analytic abilities and conclusions at the service of particular viewpoints and components within the firm.

Scale Factors in Risk Management

The political risk manager faces severe resource constraints in meeting his firm's requirements for timely and accurate assessments on foreign political developments. In a non- economic world, each firm would develop an internal capability like that of major governments for assessing foreign policies and politics and tailor those assessments to its exposure. The proliferation of in-house analytic shops modeled on the geographic or functional bureaus of the Department of State will not occur for several reasons. The key reason is the resource constraint. These governmental bureaucracies number in the thousands, with annual budgets in the millions of dollars. These resources purchase an excellent capability to track long- and short-term foreign political, economic, social, military and scientific-technical developments that effect the vital interests of the United States. But this level of effort is beyond the desire or reach of every multinational corporation and financial institution in the United States.

It is also the case that corporate executives see no reason to duplicate these governmental bureaucracies when they can have access to the wisdom of the State Department or other agencies concerned with foreign affairs. Multinationals blend their information sources, relying heavily on internal and external human sources of information, especially country or regional managers. (Kobrin, 1982) Corporate perspectives from the field are analogous to Embassy reporting and need to be seen in that context. While the State Department has long recognized the potential for going native, the multinational risk assessor should develop an institutional response to the natural bias of local management toward a rosy view. This is particularly true in initial decisions to grant loans or make large direct investments.

Each firm needs to answer the following questions in order to attain a political assessment capability that is appropriate to its needs and resources.

> Do we need a reactive or proactive assessment capability? That is, do we need a capability for continuous scanning or a capability that will produce judgments in response to events within the firm or in the international environment?
>
> Do we focus on macro-level changes in the political stability and economic performance of foreign countries?

Or, do we look only at our own firms and projects in foreign countries?

Do we use qualitative techniques of analysis and reporting or do we attempt to quantify selected factors that effect political risk?

To what extent to we rely on sources of information and expertise outside of the firm? If we rely heavily on outside resources, to what extent do we want contractors and consultants to produce finished analytic judgments or only to provide informational inputs into papers prepared by our corporate staff?

Most corporate approaches to political risk assessment are reactive in nature (Kobrin, 1982). Multinationals conduct political assessment on an ad hoc basis in response to developments within the firm (e.g., capital budgeting). One suspects that in many cases these political judgments are trundled out to support decisions already taken on other grounds rather than as an integral part of the decision- making process itself.

An alternative to the common reactive approach is to be continually scanning the foreign environment for political risks and opportunities. A continuous scanning approach will work best under the following conditions. The analysts should put bounds on his task by preparing a matrix that summarizes along one axis the exposure of the firm by foreign country and along the other axis the riskiness of each country according to the five thematic variables outlined above (economic performance, political instability, international dependence, bargaining power, impetus towards national control). Attention should be focused on those countries where the firm has the greatest exposure and where there is greatest risk. The formalization of this approach into a matrix will be resource conserving and, as updated on a quarterly basis, will provide a baseline for evaluating changes over time. Of course, the use of such a schematic matrix implies the quantification of some of the data, at least as a focusing tool.

Much attention has been paid to the distinction between macro- and micro- level political analysis. This is essentially a false distinction. While risk may be a property of a specific firm or project, factors causing risk arise out of the national environment and impact differentially on firms. That 40 percent of all nationalizations between 1960 and 1979 resulted from social revolution is one argument for paying attention to macro- level factors.

An analogy from economic analysis may help. Before introducing a new product, market research firms conduct a variety of studies to determine product acceptability. These very detailed studies cover the advertising strategy, the packaging of the product, and the appeal of the product itself to consumers. These studies on product acceptance assume an economic or commercial context that has a high level of stability. Micro-level product tests assume a given level of income, aggregate demand and availability of advertising, transportation and merchandising facilities. At a GNP of U.S. $5,000 per capita, certain appliances may sell well, but will not find a market at U.S. $4,000 per capita. Assessments of the macroeconomy provide the framework within which market researchers investigate the likely fortunes of specific products.

In the political area, opinion pollsters measure and predict individual-level behavior within a context that is shaped by macro-level variables. At the sharp end of the pollster's craft is the election forecast. These discrete events are often predicted with a high degree of accuracy from individual-level data. These individual-level data are meaningful only in the context of national norms, values, constitutional structures and electoral procedures that provide an anchoring point to judgments about the behavior of individuals. Pollsters can assume stability in the short-run characteristics of political systems. Over the longer term, changes in macro- level system properties will condition judgments about micro-level behavior.

The introduction of proactive scanning and continuing attention to macro-level properties suggests that quantitative approaches will be relevant to political risk assessment in the future. There are sound arguments for using quantitative data when these measure relevant concepts in a valid manner; are available in a reliable and timely fashion; and are known to effect political risk. The basic argument for "quantification properly understood" is that most of the questions in political risk assessment are "How Much?" questions. We are interested in the movement of variables that effect the operating environment and need to be able to measure changes over time. A simplistic coding of their absence or presence is inadequate when dealing with national economic performance and potential for political instability.

Not only do the questions push the political risk analyst in the direction of making quantitative judgments, the availabilty of reliable quantitative data provide the supply of information to meet that demand. National and international economic statistics are widely available in computerized form and political data are increasingly available on-line. National statistical data have improved over time, especially in the Third World, and are often available in a form that is conducive to making comparisons (Taylor and Jodice, 1983). Political data are available for key factors that effect risk (policy preferences of politically-active groups) as well as background data on public opinion, election results and political instability/political violence. The merging of these data with forecasting techniques based on expert judgments or econometric type models will provide a set of tools for the country risk analyst interested in a systematic, rigorous and long-term view of macro-level trends.

An additional incentive behind the use of quantitative data is the increasing understanding in private firms of the role of data and computer techniques in decision-making. While the formal incorporation of risk factors into capital budgeting models poses problems, corporate executives are accustomed to seeing problems defined in quantitative terms.

The last structural choice facing the political risk analyst is the blend of internal and external resources. We expect corporate-based analysis to rely heavily on personal contacts in the host country and impressionistic judgments based on journalistic reporting about conditions abroad. We also expect that final products, e.g., the country or regional report, will be produced in-house. Only those intimately associated with the firm can produce a report that meets its needs in a direct and focused manner. Now the question is the extent to which the firm-based analyst draws on external sources of information and assessments as input into his own writing. For an extensive treatment of the information sources available to the risk analyst, see Simon (1982).

The kinds of information services available to the corporate risk analyst vary widely in their coverage of countries and issues, their use of data, their analytic methodologies, and the degree to which their product is tailored to the specific needs of corporate clients. The modal approach is the use of expert judgment (often university-based) to present measures on variables previously determined (conceptually or empirically) to affect the vulnerability of foreign firms to political risk.

These expert judgments on components of the model are then treated as inputs into a statistical algorithm that estimates the most likely policy outcome. We describe three services below. These services were selected to represent the problems and potentials of political risk assessments techniques that are available to the corporate client.

Political Risk Services

One of the best known of the risk services is Frost and Sullivan's *World Political Risk Forecasts.* The results of this approach are disseminated in a monthly newsletter and through an on-line computer system (via NewsNet). These "currrent intelligence" type reports include an introductory section on recent developments in the domestic political and economic life of selected foreign countries, international economic and financial trends, and international political disputes. Specialized studies on such topics as international credit markets and territorial disputes are also available. Recent additions to WPRF's offerings include a database on country risk and a country-specific consulting service. For firms with wide-ranging international interests and a small internal staff, WPRF can provide much insight into foreign political and economic developments.

The WPRF workhorse is their monthly forecast of political risk in 80 countries worldwide. These forecasts are based on independent judgments from approximately 250 experts in the United States and overseas. The forecasts look forward over two time periods: 18 months and five years. The 18-month forecasts predict the regime most likely to remain or assume power within that period; the probability of political turmoil; a financial risk rating; a risk rating for expropriation in manufacturing and extractive industries; and, an export risk rating. The five-year forecast provides a single general assessment of political and economic risk and is scored with letter grades.

The core of the WPRF methodology is the use of panels of country experts, the collection of their judgments with formal questionnaires, the estimation of probabilities of political instability and expropriation with the O'Leary and Coplin PRINCE model (O'Leary and Coplin, 1981), and the use of numbers to quantify risk and its causes throughout the process. The selection of the country experts is at the heart of the enterprise. Panel members must have demonstrated experience with the country concerned, usually by study, residence or work experience; have demonstrated their ability to produce objective analyses; and are subject to continuing evaluation of their work. Anonymity is guaranteed; this goes far to increase the objectivity of the results. The political risk questionnaires elicit closed-end judgments; quantitative responses to a form covering the political disposition, power, issue preference and salience of a wide number of actors; and open-ended essays on major political figures and specific policy topics. A detailed analysis of this process and the PRINCE modelling framework is presented in Chapter I of O'Leary and Coplin (1981: pp. 7-26).

The Business Environmental Risk Index (BERI) is an alternative to WPRF. BERI measures the business climate in 45 countries around the world. BERI assesses the general quality of the business climate and the degree to which nationals are given preferential treatment. BERI's focus is different from WPRF's. BERI is less specific and covers fewer countries.

BERI's estimates are derived from expert opinion also. Approximately 100 experts provide judgments on 15 criteria within the general categories of political stability and governmental efficiency; financial well-being of the country; operational factors affecting business (e.g., currency convertibility, enforcement of contracts); and, nationalism. BERI undertakes the same pains to maintain quality, consistency and objectivity of its expert panel as does WPRF.

BERI's final product includes specific scores like those of WPRF, but the basic conclusions are often modified on the basis of a separately derived political risk index (built up by political scientists rather than government or business executives) and the opinion of BERI's staff. The BERI staff opinion is a judgmental coding on the riskiness of the 45 countries derived from staff expertise in general.

A very promising new effort in the political risk area is POLICON -- an offering of Data Resources, Inc. (DRI). Like WPRF and BERI, POLICON is based on expert judgments about foreign political and economic conditions. Like WPRF, POLICON is available on-line through DRI's software network (EPS). Unlike either WPRF or BERI, DRI enables users to access system data on variables in the model (see below) or provide their own judgments about conditions affecting political risk. In certain cases customers may have access to information that is superior to that of DRI's panel. More frequently, we expect that customers will want to test alternative scenarios of policymaking. Altering the basic input data in a customer specific file will allow different iterations of the POLICON model.

The core of the POLICON approach is a expected utility model that explains the behavior of groups within the political system of a given country. Experts code the issue preferences of various groups, sub-groups and individuals; assess the level of economic, political and military resources these groups are able to bring to bear in the political process; and, judge the salience of the issue to each group. The POLICON model then calculates the most likely policy outcome taking into consideration second, third and nth group interactions of a cooperative and conflictual nature.

Significantly, the POLICON framework does not ask experts to judge the likelihood of political risk. They are not asked to state whether there will be an expropriation or not. The experts are asked to estimate the components of the model (issues, groups, issue salience, group resources) on a country, group and issue specific basis. The POLICON model calculates the most likely outcome. DRI has found that the experts are more likely to be objective, consistent and reliable when asked to estimate background variables than when they are asked to predict discrete policy actions.

The DRI approach differs from both WPRF and BERI because it presents a database and model (in addition to client-oriented consulting) that can be tailored to very specific policy predictions. This is the kind of micro-level tool that the profession has been looking for to supplement system-oriented approaches. With POLICON, the corporate political risk analyst can estimate the likelihood of specific policies effecting individual firms or projects as well as general changes in the national environment. He can also conduct sensitivity tests of the model and run alternative scenarios. The degree to which the predicted outcome changes in response to different mixes of input data is a measure of the confidence that the analyst can have in his predictions. The DRI-POLICON approach is not without its limitations. Its focus is short- term. But, so are those of WPRF and BERI, not to mention most decision-makers. POLICON tells the risk analyst little about long-term trends in political stability and how issues and groups come to the fore. POLICON, WPRF and BERI need to be supplemented by long-term forecasting techniques.

Prospects for the Future

The future promises both increased demand for and supply of political risk assessment. The demand for an understanding of foreign political environments will continue to increase with the involvement of U.S. corporations and financial institutions in foreign countries, particularly the Third World. The increasing significance of the Third World as a market for U.S. exports, a location for U.S. manufacturing investment, and as a debtor to Western banks, indicates no decline in the need for corporate-based political analysis. Of course, effective demand (measured in terms of positions and resources committed to political risk) may lag behind real corporate needs.

The supply of political risk analysts will be more than sufficient to meet demand. Supply will expand through the introduction of political scientists into business and the training of existing corporate officers as risk analysts. Quality control will continue to be a concern. At the individual level differences will be identified through conventional professional means (e.g., the Association of Political Risk Analysts). The professionalism and accuracy of the risk services can only be assessed over time by comparing forecasts with real outcomes. There has been a large gap in this area. It is incumbent on consumers of risk services to demand an evaluation of the track record. The risk services, for varying reasons, are unlikely to supply such comparisons in the absence of customer demand.

The declining real cost of collecting and processing political and economic data will, when combined with relatively inexpensive and easy to use computer equipment, will strengthen the quantitative side of political risk assessment. Corporate executives and staff professionals are increasingly numerate and will accept political and social data if these can be shown to be as relevant and reliable as the economic and financial data that they are accustomed to using. Demand for explicit comparisons (over time and across countries) will facilitate the use of computerized data in evaluating country risk.

The data do not speak for themselves, however. The application of explicit modelling routines (e.g., POLICON) to expert generated data appears to be one of the most fruitful avenues for progress. The matching of interest group preferences with their resources and issue positions allows the analyst to estimate likely policy choices and investigate the changes that would have to occur in key variables in order to realize different policies. The durability of predicted outcomes relative to changes in input variables is one indicator of the confidence that one can place in the predictions. A superior indicator, and an exogenous one, is the comparison of the predictions with reality.

Macro-level system studies of economic performance and political stability will be used as background data. These set the bounds within which micro-level policy decisions are reached and within which risk effects specific firms and projects. For longer-term planning (e.g., large resource or manufacturing investments; long-term loans), econometric forecasting methodologies are an essential supplement to the current or short-term perspectives offered by techniques based on expert judgment.

Chapter Two: The Multinational Corporation in World Politics

Adelman, Morris A. *The World Petroleum Market.* **Baltimore: Johns Hopkins University Press, 1972, p. 438.**

This study focuses on the economics of international oil and is keyed to the factors that determine the real price of crude. The industry was characterized by a gap between the cost of production and the selling price which, combined with new entrants into the industry, produced a declining real price for crude until 1971.

Adelman marshalls much theory and evidence to debunk the common notion that the marginal price of oil at the wellhead is zero. Putting numbers to theory, he estimates the cost of producing marginal barrels of oil. Working in the early 1970s, Adelman predicts increasing conflicts as host governments become more involved in the petroleum business through regulation, expropriation and the operation of state-owned oil companies. The excellent economic analysis is supplemented by abundant data and technical appendices.

Agmon, Tamir and Charles P. Kindleberger (eds.). *Multinationals from Small Countries.* **Cambridge, Mass.: MIT Press, 1977, p. 224.**

This collection of articles is based on a conference held at MIT during January 1976 to explore the growth of multinational companies from small home countries. Small countries are those lacking substantial international power (Switzerland, Sweden, Australia, selected less developed countries). The various authors review the benefits of multinational expansion for the home country, compare government policies that favor international expansion, and the effects of such expansion on technology transfer and financial flows.

Among others, Louis Wells examines the internationalization of firms from developing countries, Diaj-Alejandro discusses the foreign direct investment of firms based in Latin America. The authors conclude that the search for economies of scale is a major force behind the internationalization of firms from small countries.

Aharoni, Yair, and Clifford Baden. ***Business in the International Environment.*** **Boulder: Westview Press, 1977, p. 245.**

Increasing concern about environmental analysis (read country risk assessment) is pushing businessmen toward political science, macroeconomic analysis and technological forecasting. The cutting edge of environmental analysis is the increasing role of government in economic affairs. Aharoni and Baden argue for a specific approach to environmental assessment. They begin by identifying the actors that are relevant to policymaking. They next identify the issue positions of those actors, the resources they bring to bear on policymaking and the interaction among these politically active forces. Environmental analysis should be conducted on a regular basis as an ongoing function of the firm. The authors provide several case studies on the role of interest groups in decisionmaking, techniques for assessing risks and opportunities, and the role of the firm in the national community.

Ball, George W. (ed.). ***Global Companies: The Political Economy of World Business.*** **Englewood Cliffs, N. J: Prentice-Hall, 1975, p. 179.**

This anthology presents original articles by leading scholars of the multinational enterprise. The editor and Eugene V. Rostow present an analysis of the rise of the multinational corporation. Ball examines host country policies and, with Seymour J. Rubin, looks at home government policies toward outward foreign direct investment. Charles P. Kindleberger contributes a piece on the multinational company in a world of militant developing countries. Herbert Salzman writes of techniques for managing and reducing political risk in developing countries. Another article by Rostow comments on the role of multinationals in the future world economy while Joseph S. Nye and Rubin assess the longer range international political role of the multinational. This work is of use to the general student of international affairs as well as those focusing on political risk assessment.

Barnett, Richard J., and Ronald E. Muller. *Global Reach: The Power of Multinational Corporations.* **New York: Simon and Schuster, 1974, p. 508.**

Barnett and Muller present a substantial study on the causes and effects of multinational expansion beyond the United States. Managers of multinational corporations are characterized as world managers, the latest in a long series of world conquerors. Their stature is based on the shrinking of the world in terms of transportation and communication costs, the world view of corporate management itself; and corporate size and centralization.

World corporations do not go unchallenged, however. Principal among their antagonists are organized labor, politicians and bureaucracies in host countries, and the loosely described younger generation.

The authors describe the types of people who inhabit the multinational corporation, the ways and means by which they exercise diplomatic and political power, their effects on U.S. foreign policy and their political activities at the local level. While the authors are quick to blame multinational corporations for much of the world's ills, they fail to consider what a world without such business firms would be like. The timing of the book and the author's own political values explain much of this bias in description and explanation.

Bauer, Raymond A., Ithiel De Sola Pool, and Lewis A. Dexter. *American Business and Public Policy.* **Chicago: Aldine-Atherton, 1972, p. 499.**

The purpose of this study is to contribute to the reader's understanding of ""decision- making, communication and democratic processes"" (xx). Through extensive interviews the authors examine the relations of the Congress with business groups. They develop a complex framework to explain Congressional reaction to business claims for special treatment. Congressmen act to maximize the probability over many decisions of returning to Capitol Hill. With time the scarcest commodity, they select the issues and problems to which they will respond. These processes are examined in the area of foreign trade policy. The history of U.S. foreign trade policy is presented, the positions of businesses, eight selected communities and the opinion of the public at large are reviewed.

Behrman, Jack N. *National Interest and the Multinational Enterprise.* **Englewood Cliffs, N.J: Prentice-Hall, 1970, p. 194.**

As a former Assistant Secretary of State, the author brings both academic and applied concerns to this analysis of the impact of multinational corporations on national economic objectives. The book focuses on the postwar experience of U.S. and West European manufacturing companies in industrial societies.

Behrman explains how the initial welcome extended by the host country wanes after the benefits of new foreign direct investment (capital, technology, management skills, regional development) are offset by disadvantageous balance of payments effects and competition with local industry. The fears of the host country include industrial concentration and domination of local industry by foreign firms, technological dependence, conflicts with national economic plans.

Policy options for host countries include entry regulations, behavioral controls, local private or state ownership, the strengthening of domestic industry and international agreements. In terms of outward foreign direct investment, the U.S. has adopted a mix of policies over time including antitrust, technology controls, and restrictions on the movements of capital.

Bergsten, C. Fred and Lawrence B. Krause. (eds.). *World Politics and International Economics.* **Washington, D.C: Brookings Institution, 1975, p. 359.**

This compendium was originally published as the Winter 1975 edition of *International Organization.* It includes sections on models for analyzing international political and economic change. As presented by Robert Gilpin, these models are characterized as marxist, mercantilist (state-centric) and liberal (pluralist). These models specify the relationship between state and society, the degree of state autonomy in the area of international policymaking, and the basic objectives of states in the international system. Other contributions focus on specific issue areas: the international monetary system, the international regulation of multinational corporations, trade and the GATT, and foreign aid. Economic relations between North and South, South and South, and East and West are also analyzed. A select bibliography is also included.

Bergsten, Fred C., Thomas Horst and Theodore H. Moran. *American Multinationals and American Interests.* **Washington D.C: Brookings Institution, 1978, p. 535.**

The central theme of this extensive study is the effect of U.S.-based multinationals on the US economy and foreign policy. The basic argument is that the U.S. has traditionally not had a policy toward multinationals per se, but has affected multinationals through policies developed in other contexts: trade promotion, economic development, balance of payments financing and employment policy. The book is organized into sections that review the literature, study the key issues, develop case studies, and review American policy in the following areas: balance of payments, access to raw materials, taxation, industrial structure/antitrust, and foreign policy in general toward developed and developing countries alike.

The purpose of the book is a prescriptive one. The authors propose several changes in U.S. policy toward US-based multinational corporations. First, that the U.S. tax system be neutral with respect to foreign operations. Tax policies should not be used to subsidize or penalize U.S. companies operating overseas. Second, the authors recommend that the U.S. government broaden the scope of its adjustment assistance beyond jobs to other factors affected by the foreign operations of U.S. multinationals. Third, the authors propose an alternative criteria for the application of antitrust law. The focus of antitrust policy should move from the intent to monopolize to the effects of monopolization. The fourth major proposal is to restructure the insurance activities of OPIC, the quasi-public Overseas Private Investment Corporation. Although the portfolio will be a high-risk one, Bergsten, Horst and Moran argue that OPIC would be more effective if if focused on Fourth World countries and the resource extraction sector in particular. Such a radical change in the nature and scale of OPIC's exposure would necessitate a new understanding with the Congress about the risk bearer of last resort. Lastly, the authors propose that the U.S. adopt a flexible policy toward nationalizing governments in the developing areas. This proposal seems already to be in effect.

Biersteker, Thomas J. *Distortion or Development: Contending Perspectives on the Multinational Corporation.* **Cambridge, Mass: MIT Press, 1978, p. 199.**

Biersteker presents two perspectives on the multinational corporation in the developing world. The first is critical of the multinational corporation because of its negative effects, on balance, on indigenous production, technology transfer, consumption patterns in the host country, changes in social structure and income inequality. The alternative perspective, the neoconventional or Harvard Business School approach, is favorable to the multinational enterprise because of its putative positive effects on host country welfare and economic development. Biersteker develops testable propositions to contrast these two schools and evaluates these propositions at the micro level in Nigeria.

The Nigerian case study is based on interviews with 60 foreign and domestic firms incorporated in the country between 1963 and 1972. Approximately 300 executives were interviewed. Interview results were supplemented by firm-specific data from the Federal Office of Statistics and the Central Bank of Nigeria. The author used statistical techniques such as multiple regression to evaluate his hypotheses about th effects of foreign direct investment on the host economy.

Biersteker concludes that there was little outright displacement of existing local firms by foreign investors. Multinationals have effectively transferred knowledge and skills to the host economy, mainly through the application of techniques that are more capital-intensive than those in use in the indigenous economy. The author also concludes that multinationals also introduce inappropriate production methods. This is difficult to reconcile with the desire on the part of host countries for more advanced technology which, by definition, is labor conserving.

Blair, John M. ***The Control of Oil.*** **New York: Vintage Books, 1976, p. 441.**

Writing in the context of an energy short world, Blair is highly critical of the international oil industry. He argues that it is a monopoly whose control over production and pricing has been abetted by governments of consuming and producing countries. As evidence, he cites the vertical integration of the industry, its high concentration, cartel agreements and government intervention through state ownership or policy actions.

Blair belongs to the school that considers the wellhead price of oil to equal zero at the margin. Consequently, his analysis looks to the activities of cartels (companies or producing governments) to maintain the real price of oil. Supply of foreign oil has been controlled at the source and through marketing arrangements. Despite the postwar growth of oil independents, Blair maintains that outsiders have been excluded from the industry. On the U.S. domestic side, oil has been controlled through prorationing (i.e., the Texas Railroad Commission), and the use of oil import quotas. The net effect of these measures has been to price U.S. domestic oil above the world price (until 1973) and to hasten the depletion of U.S. continental reserves.

Bock, P.G., and Vincent J. Fuccillo. "Transnational Corporations as International Political Actors." *Studies in Comparative International Development.* **10 (1975): 51-74.**

This article describes the growth of multinational corporations in the context of the general growth of non-state actors in world affairs. The multinational corporation is defined, a typology of corporations is presented and their characteristics are described. Relations between multinationals and their home governments are reviewed. The international political impact of multinationals is assessed in terms of their influence on interactions between nation-states and the structure of the international system.

Brooke, Michael Z., and H. Lee Remmers (eds.). *The Multinational Corporation in Europe: Some Key Problems.* **London: Longman Group, Ltd. 1972, p. 194.**

This study covers the growth of the international economy since World War II and the changing role of multinational corporations in the international economic system. Written with the multinational manager in mind, the book discussed how financial strategy is determined in foreign operations, accounting practices, the role of the national manager in a multinational enterprise, American-European joint ventures in Western Europe. A major question is whether Americans can learn from European managers. Brooke compares the education, culture and management style of American, French, British and Israeli managers.

Brooke, Michael Z., and H. Lee Remmers. ***The Strategy of Multinational Enterprise.*** **London: Pitman Publishing Company, 1978, p. 389.**

This text examines techniques for control and decisionmaking in multinational corporations. It assesses relations between the head office, regional offices and local management. Communication systems, decisionmaking methods, financial control systems and the impact of personalities are discussed. A second major section deals with expansion strategies and the external environment. This is of more direct interest to the political risk analyst. Specifically, Brooke and Remmers look at decisions to invest or not invest, government relations strategies and ownership policies.

Buckley, Peter J., and Mark Casson. ***The Future of Multinational Enterprise.*** **New York: Holmes and Meier, 1976, p. 116.**

This study focuses on the foreign activity of U.S.-based manufacturing firms since World War II. Factors derived driving the outward expansion of American corporations are analyzed with data from the Harvard Multinational Enterprise Project. The growth of MNCs are determined by the costs and benefits of "internalizing" external markets. Alternative theories of multinational expansion are compared and tested with data on approximately 400 U.S. firms.

After World War II the international movement of investment capital took off. Most of this was between capital intensive economies with similar demand structures, in contrast to the expectations derived from international economic theory. Multinationals tended to be larger than the average firm, more capital-intensive, in concentrated industries, with high research and development expenditures and skilled staffs. These generalizations are supported by an econometric analysis of 434 international subsidiaries in comparison with 170 large U.S. domestic firms.

Caporaso, James (ed.). ***Dependence and Dependency in the Global System: Special Edition of International Organization.*** **32 (1) (Winter 1978): p. 300.**

This theme issue of *International Organization* focuses on the definitions, measurement and explanations of dependence and dependency in the international system. The collection starts off with overview chapters by Raymond Duvall, Caporaso and Theodore Moran. These chapters are concerned, respectively, with distinctions between dependence and dependency theory, the structural and behavioral analyses of dependency in the Third World, and the effects of multinational corporations on dependence.

Case studies examine specific instances of dependent linkages. Lynn Mytelka examines the technological dependence of the Andean Group. Patrick McGowan analyzes the level and forms of international dependence among Black African states. Gary Gereffi presents an analysis on the international dependence of the pharmaceutical industry in Mexico.

Chandler, Geoffrey. "The Myth of Oil Power, International Groups and National Sovereignty."" *International Affairs.* **46 (October 1970).**

Contrary to much academic wisdom in the 1970s, Chandler argues with effect that although the role of multinational companies has expanded in world affairs, the role of the nation-state in the oil industry has grown and its sovereignty remains unimpaired. As evidence, Chandler offers the record on the nationalization of oil investments throughout the Third World since the early 1970s (and before for selected countries), and the increasing share of governments in crude oil production, refining and marketing. These observations encompass the role of state oil companies in Western Europe and among the centrally-planned economies. Governments are not unrestrained, however. According to Chandler, their objectives are frustrated by the internationalization of oil supply and demand, rather than by the activities of private oil companies *per se*.

Channon, Derek F. with Michael Jallard. ***Multinational Strategic Planning.*** **New York: AMA Communications Division, 1978, p. 344.**

Multinational corporations are defined and their evolution is described. The changing nature of multinational planning systems is analyzed. Organiztional approaches are reviewed in terms of different types of structures: export sales, international divisions, global functional structures, and worldwide product division structures. Portfolio planning and corporate treasury management are also reviewed.

Church, Frank. "The Impotence of Oil Companies." ***Foreign Policy.*** **27 (Summer 1977): 27-51.**

Senator Church argued that the international oil companies are now the instruments rather than the initiators of OPEC oil policy. Citing the December 1976 Saudi decision to hold down the real price of crude, Church discusses how the majors (Exxon, Mobil, Texaco and Socal) were used to carry out that decision. He asks: Are U.S. oil companies any longer susceptible to U.S. foreign policy control? Or, is their stake in Saudi Arabia so great that they have become mere instruments of Saudi foreign policy - "rather than our own"? Fearing the worst, Senator Church argued for a restructuring of incentives facing the U.S.-based oil companies to encourage the development of non-OPEC oil.

Cole, Constance K. "American Multinationals: Global Impacts of and Adaptations to Changes in the International Commodity Regime." *Paper Presented at the Annual Meeting of the American Political Science Association.* **(Denver, September 2-5, 1982), p. 42.**

This paper reviews the activity of U.S.-based multinationals engaged in agribusiness in Latin America. It discusses the context of U.S. policymaking in the late 1970s and early 1980s on the promotion and protection of foreign direct investment in Latin America. Declining investment in agriculture (related in part to extensive nationalizations of foreign-owned farms) led to Latin America becoming a net food importer. Trade data tables are also presented.

Connelly, Philip and Robert Perlman. *The Politics of Scarcity: Resource Conflicts in International Relations.* **London: Oxford University Press, 1975, p. 162.**

Connelly and Perlman focus on non-renewable resources in their analysis of the political and economic implications of resource scarcity. They are concerned, in part, with the market influence and international political power that flow from absolute local control over key commodities. Writing after the first OPEC shock, they argue that the scarcity of resources substantially increases the bargaining power of resource producing countries. Two major recessions later, the availability of downstream processing facilities and markets are evident as important constraints on the bargaining power of resource producers.

Resource producers are comparable in their behavior toward foreign enterprises in several ways. The first item is their tendency to form commodity cartels (e.g., OPEC, CIPEC, IBA) in order to control production and price. These cartels also serve as a forum for comparing agreements across countries. Second, they use independents to limit the influence of the majors by stimulating competition. Third, the (threat of) nationalization of direct investments can lead to higher participation ratios and greater real return. The power of commodity cartels are determined by their share of the world market, the price and availablity of alternatives, common institutions and shared political values.

Returning to their central theme, Connelly and Perlman argue that technology will solve the major problems facing resource producers and consumers. Scarcity is a dynamic property whose frontiers are being pushed back in the areas of exploration, extraction, substitution and environmental impact.

Curzon, Gerard; and Victoria Curzon (eds.), with the collaboration of Lawrence G. Franko and Henri Schwam. ***The Multinational Enterprise in a Hostile World.*** **London: Macmillan Press, 1972, p. 147.**

This collection was based on a conference held at the Graduate Institute of International Studies, University of Geneva. It focuses on the role of multinational corporations in the European Community. Specific topics include the effects of multinationals on the integration process, the industrial competitiveness policies of the EC, restrictionist policies of the multinationals themselves, and the limits and possibilities of antitrust.

Daniels, John D., Ernest W. Ogram, Jr., and Lee H. Radebaugh. *International Business: Environments and Operations.* **Reading, Mass: Addison-Wesley, 1976, p. 703.**

This basic text provides an overview of international trade theory, an assessment of the reasons behind foreign investment, and a review of the historical setting of international business. Topics include the world financial environment, foreign exchange, international payments, financial markets and taxation. Special attention (pp. 187–292) is devoted to international business in a nationalistic world and examines sources of conflict in trade and investment. The section on operations includes research for international decisions (e.g., the "political climate") and information on personnel management, compensation, marketing, and forms of investment.

Davis, Stanley M. "Trends in the Organization of Multinational Corporations." *Columbia Journal of World Business.* **11(2), (Summer 1976): 59–71.**

In this theme issue on changing corporate structures, Davis comments that worldwide functional structures are showing instability. Corporations that are organized by country are working to place product management more effectively within that structure. Firms with worldwide product groups require better coordination. Few have experimented with global matrix management.

Dunning, John H. (ed.). ***Economic Analysis and the Multinational Enterprise.*** **London: George Allen and Unwin, 1974, p. 405.**

This substantial edited collection deals with the determinants of investments, location of economic activities, industrial organization, technology transfer, monetary policy, development policy, wage rates and collective bargaining and the effects of multinational corporations on income distribution and welfare. Each contributor surveys the field in his area, examines the implications of multinational corporations for economic analysis, summarizes the major theories in the field as well as the empirical research, and presents his own views on changes needed to theory and avenues for future research.

Dunning, John H. ***International Production and the Multinational Enterprise.*** **London: George Allen and Unwin, 1981, p. 439.**

This book is a collection of previously published, but revised articles. Topics include definitions of the multinational enterprise, theories of international trade, investment and plant location, and an analysis of the international trade posture of the UK in the mid-1970s. Dunning tracks the effects of multinational enterprises on industrial policy, domestic capital formation, locational strategies/regional development plans, trade flows of developing countries, employee compensation and technology transfer.

Dunning presents a "tool kit" for evaluating the costs and benefits of multinational enterprises to the host country (pp. 357-86). The criteria include effects on the macroeconomy, national sovereignty, distributional equity and participation in economic decision-making. The effects of foreign direct investment should be assessed net of the release of domestic resources for other purposes. The development of "what if" scenarios should put the foreign enterprise in perspective.

Dunning, John H. ***The Multinational Enterprise.*** **New York: Praeger Publishers, 1971, p. 368.**

This symposium of American and British economists examines the effects of the multinational enterprise on national welfare through their movements of goods,services and factors across national borders. Topics include the growth of multinational enterprise, the international transfer of technology, the impact of multinationals on organized labor, effects on trade flows and trade policy when international trade occurs as intrafirm transfers, and the costs and benefits of multinational enterprises in developing countries.

The Economist. ***The Growth and Spread of Multinational Companies.*** **London: The Economist Intelligence Unit, 1971, p. 80.**

This study presents data on the outward expansion of U.S.-based manufacturing firms from 1929–1969. It is based on U.S. Department of Commerce data. Multinational corporations have advantages over local competitors through their production facilities, research and development staffs, their marketing networks and worldwide flexibility. Multinational corporations are catalysts for structural change in national markets.

Multinationals have prompted strong responses from the governments and labor unions of many host countries, particularly in the Third World. These nationalizations in the Third World are due to political as well as economic factors. "In Africa, there has been a round of competitive nationalisations, whereby a political leader finds he can buy off potential domestic unrest by channelling popular dissatisfaction against the foreigners who own the country's basic industries." (p. 46.) Other sections deal with the response to foreign investment of developed host countries - Japan, Canada, France and Great Britain.

Fayerweather, John (ed.). *International Business-Government Affairs.* **Cambridge, Mass: Ballinger Publishing Company, 1973, p. 134.**

The contributors to this symposium argue that the confrontational era of government - multinational relations is over. An era of negotiation will replace an era of conflict over ownership of resources throughout the Third World. This outlook is based on the following considerations.

Basic attitudes toward the multinational are changing. Although the mass public has a diffuse hostility to the foreign firm, because the nation-state as the key decision-maker for the society is seen as threatened by the multinational, there is a growing acceptance of the multinational corporation at the elite level. The development of genuinely transnational corporations will diffuse hostility formerly directed at firms from the major powers. A more assertive control of foreign business entry will reduce conflict later on in the life of the investment. Greater attention by management to the political and social life of the host country will also ease conflict.

Fayerweather, John. *International Business Management: A Conceptual Framework.* **New York: McGraw-Hill, 1969, p. 220.**

Sources of political risk lie in the greater integration of direct investment compared to export sales; conflicts between national interests and a global business strategy; and relations with social forces in the host society. Multinationals affect host countries through technology transfer, a movement of resources (capital, skills, management) into the country, and a diffusion of innovation. Innovative methods can affect the authority and value systems of the host country, the pattern of income distribution and consumption, the relationship of labor to capital, and the ability of the government to manage the national economy.

Fayerweather, John, and Ashok Kapoor. *Strategy and Negotiation for the International Corporation: Guidelines and Cases.* **Cambridge, Mass: Ballinger Publishing Company, 1976, p. 456.**

This study provides an overview for the foreign investor on techniques for negotiating with individuals, firms and governmental organizations. The text illustrates the interaction of the commercial climate and government policy in shaping the negotiation process.

Feld, Werner J. *Multinational Corporations and U.N. Politics: The Quest for Codes of Conduct.* **New York: Pergamon Press, 1980.**

Conflict between host governments and multinationals is due, largely, to the loss of national economic control and competition with indigenous firms when there is large-scale foreign direct investment. Specific problem areas discussed in this book are: balance of payments, employment, technology transfer, transfer pricing and taxation, effects of multinational behavior on host government macroeconomic policies, extraterritorial application of home government laws, and attempts by multinationals to influence local politics.

Feld reviews the history of efforts to define a code of conduct within the U.N. beginning with the formation in 1973 of the Group of Eminent Persons and the establishment in 1974 of the Centre on Transnational Corporations. The U.N. code is compared to that proposed by the International Chamber of Commerce and the OECD.

The Third World does not speak with one voice in the area of codes of conduct for multinational corporations. Members of OPEC and the NICs (Newly Industrializing Countries) have interests that are increasingly divergent from other developing countries or those in the "Fourth World." Bargaining power is shifting away from hosts in the developing areas as wage differentials narrow and the growth of capital slows in the industrial countries. These factors, plus the indebtedness of many host countries, undermine the attractiveness of investing in the Third World.

Freeman, Orville L. *The Multinational Company: Instrument for World Power.* **New York: Praeger Publishers, 1981, p. 127.**

This short book is based on the speeches and papers of the author who is the President of Business International. He is responding to critics of the multinationals but recognizes the need for flexibility in adapting to conditions in the host country. Freeman reviews the purpose and benefits of multinationals, the effects of multinationals on host country sovereignty and economic growth, and the institutions to which the multinational is accountable. Freeman argues that the multinational is accountable to its employees and shareholders, but overlooks demands for accountability to customers, suppliers or society as a whole.

Gabriel, Peter P. "The Investment in the LDC: Asset with a Fixed Maturity." *Columbia Journal of World Business.* **1 (Summer 1966): 109–19.**

Gabriel argues that the continued growth of developing countries depends on their ability to attract the skills, technologies and resources of the industrial nations. The traditional carrier of those assets has been foreign direct investment by multinational companies. When faced by political risk or economic nationalism in the developing countries, companies can leave, try to change the environment, or adapt to changing circumstances. Gabriel argues that several global changes have altered the context of foreign investment. The abandonment of the gold standard has shifted the burden of economic adjustment from the domestic to the international sector. This is particularly true under floating exchange rates. This focuses attention on the activities of multinationals because of their effects on international capital movements and exchange balances. Over time, bargaining power has shifted in the direction of host states in the Third World. Gabriel advises that multinational managers regard their investments in the Third World as impermanent. The duration of the investment will depend on firm specific attributes as well as characteristics of the host country. Gabriel leaves, overall, a negative impression about the degree of risk. However, when the piece was written it was a useful corrective to over-optimism about doing business in the Third World on the basis of traditional norms. Had Gabriel's warnings been more generally heeded, there would have been fewer surprises as the pace of nationalization quickened after 1968.

Gilpin, Robert. *U.S. Power and the Multinational Corporation: The Political Economy of Foreign Direct Investment.* **New York: Basic Books, 1975, p. 291.**

Gilpin focuses on models of international political economy and evaluates their relevance to U.S. policy toward outward foreign direct investment. Like Britain in the nineteenth-century, the U.S. has since 1945 provided an umbrella under which U.S.-based corporations could expand into the developing areas as well as Western Europe. U.S. political and economic hegemony explains the outward expansion of U.S. capitalism as much as its technological superiority, search for markets or economies of scale.

Gilpin's choice of a mercantilist or state-centric analytic framework (over liberal or Marxist theories) parallels his policy prescriptions. He cautions that the U.S. must not commit Britain's strategic economic error: investing overseas to the detriment of the home economy. A declining industrial power like the U.S. has four strategic options: foreign portfolio investment; foreign direct investment; rejuvenation of the domestic economy; and closure against the outside world. Closure is not a viable option given U.S. dependence on critical minerals and, to a lesser extent, oil from outside its borders. However, as a large continental power with a traditionally small trade sector, the U.S. has strategic economic options that were unavailable to Great Britain.

Green, Robert T., and Christopher M. North. "Political Instability and the Foreign Investor." ***California Management Review*****. 17(1), (Fall 1974): 23-31.**

Green and Korth argue that the most dramatic and consequential forms of political risk arise from political instability in the host country. As a consequence of political risk, corporate executives pay attention to political instability. Three measures of political instability developed by academic political scientists are presented and discussed. Bruce M. Russett presented two measures drawn from data in the first edition of the *World Handbook of Political and Social Indicators.*

These were deaths from political violence per one million population and a measure of executive stability (length of term). Arthur Banks and Robert Textor present a qualitative measure of governmental stability. They distinguish political systems according to the presence or absence of non- constitutional change in governments since World War I and World War II. The most stable polities are those that have not experienced non-constitutional changes in government since World War I. The Feierabends present a three-digit score based on the occurrence of 30 different types of political events ranging from peaceful protest to revolution.

While these measures, and others, drawn from political science are important for measuring political instability, their relationship to political risk has not been shown. A conceptual framework is lacking for the integration of political instability measures into political risk assessment. There has also been no empirical validation of the relationship between these measures and instances of political risk.

Grieves, Forest L. (ed.). ***Transnationalism in World Politics and Business.*** **New York: Pergamon Press, 1979, p. 214.**

This edited collection is at the border of political science and international business. It discusses transnationalism as a concept that is relatively new to the study of international affairs. It reviews the impact of transnational ties by examining multinationals and the political process, codes of conduct for multinationals, and the transnationalization of domestic policies (e.g., ties between U.S. and West European policy on social security.) OPEC is, of course, another transnational phenomena that is analyzed from the point of view of Arab development. Several strains resulting from transnationalism are also reviewed. These include the role of the World Bank, imperialism as a system of privilege, nationalization of British investors by China

(1949–57), the role of the German Democratic Republic in the communist penetration of Africa, and Dutch foreign policy between 1973 and 1974. Although this is a disparate collection, the student of political risk will be well served by Thomas N. Thompson's article on the Shanghai nationalizations as well as the prefatory material on transnationalism and world politics.

Hahlo, H. R., J. Graham and Richard W. Wright (eds.). *Nationalism and the Multinational Enterprise: Legal, Economic, and Managerial Aspects.* **Dobbs Ferry, New York: Oceana Publications, 1973, p. 373.**

This edited collection is based on a 1971 conference at the Institute of Comparative Law, McGill University. The contributors analyze the multinational enterprise in a variety of national settings: United States, Great Britain, Canada, West Germany, Africa, and the European Community generally. Specific topics include the cost and benefits of multinational corporations to host countries, the management of the multinational enterprise, litigation and arbitration, and antitrust law in the U.S., Canada and Western Europe.

Hawkins, Robert G., and Ingo Walter. "The Multinational Corporation," pp. 159–98 in Ryan C. Amacher, Gottfried Haberler and Thomas D. Willett (eds.). *Challenges to a Liberal International Order.* **Washington,D.C: American Enterprise Institute, 1979.**

Multinational corporations are the central elements shaping interdependence. They have taken the brunt of increasingly vocal challenges to an interdependent world order in both home and host countries. This study reviews the activity and structure of U.S.

multinationals in the world economy, assesses their competitive strengths and effects on global economic welfare and efficiency.

Areas of conflict from the home country's point of view are job displacement, erosion of technological advantages and the capital base; inequitable and inefficient taxation, anti-competitive practices; and the complication of domestic economic policies. For the host country the effects of foreign investment are observed in the balance of payments, taxation, employment and technology transfer. Options for national control include entry controls, limiting multinationals to certain sectors or ownership structures, operating controls (domestic content, export shares, wage rates, etc.) and financial controls over profit repatriation.

Huntington, Samuel P. "Transnational Organizations in World Politics." *World Politics.* **25(3), (April 1973): 333-68.**

Huntington writes of a "transnational organization revolution" changing the character of international relations in the last half of the twentieth-century. These transnational organizations are large, hierarchically structured bureaucracies (Catholic Church, U.S. Air Force, General Motors). They perform a limited set of functions and operate across one or more international boundaries. They may be governmental or non-governmental, bureaucratic or transactional. Transnational corporations are, according to Huntington, a uniquely American legacy based on U.S. technical capacity and political access to foreign societies.

Hymer, Stephen. *The International Operation of National Firms: A Study of Foreign Direct Investment.* **Cambridge: MIT Press, 1976, p. 253.**

This study is the posthumously published version of Hymer's doctoral dissertation for MIT's Department of Economics. It compares direct and portfolio investment, presents a theory of portfolio investment, assesses the applicability of that theory to direct investment, and develops a theory of foreign direct investment. Hymer's theory of international operations includes an analysis of barriers to investment abroad, the removal of conflict as a cause of investment abroad, diversification as a reason for investment and the possession of advantages (skills, capital, technology) as an incentive for investing in foreign environments. This work emphasizes the advantages of the multinational company and presents an aggressive picture of investment strategy. Risks facing the foreign investor and defensive motivations for overseas investment (competition, import barriers) receive less attention.

Jacoby, Neil H. ***Multinational Oil: A Study in Industry Dynamics.*** **New York: Macmillan Publishing Company, 1974, p. 323.**

This introductory text reviews the character of the oil industry, the role of energy in daily life, the nature of demand for energy and oil in particular, and the determinants of the structure of the industry. Jacoby charts the development of the industry in layman's terms. Major developments include U.S. entry into foreign oil production, the postwar explosion of consumption (mostly of gasoline), an even greater increase in the supply of foreign oil, and new entrants into the oil business. These new entrants were a diverse lot ranging from American independents to the state-owned companies from Western Europe, and the Soviet Union.

Rising governmental intervention in the oil business was noted by Jacoby in both the area of equity ownership (nationalization and expropriation) and behavioral regulation (exploration, development, downstream processing, marketing). Jacoby attributes this increase in state activism to host perceptions of foreign dominance of the oil industry, the ratio of domestic consumption to total oil production (i.e. is the oil sector a foreign exchange earner?) and the availability of domestic coal as a substitute for oil. Aside from these nationally-specific factors, global inflation, rising nationalism and the Arab-Israeli conflict affected all sectors of the petroleum industry during the 1970s.

Jacoby, Neil, H., Peter Nehemkis, and Richard Eells. *Bribery and Extortion in World Business.* **New York: Macmillan, 1977, p. 294.**

Both sides of corrupt practices are presented in this original and refreshing treatment. Corrupt practices are composed of attempts by (foreign) business to bribe local officials *and* attempts by host government officials to extort financial or other favors from the businessman. The authors characterized the corrupt practices situation in market terms; they depict both the demand for and the supply of political influence. Demand for political influence is affected by the size of the country's economy, the extent of governmental regulation of the economy, and the degree of uncertainty in the government's administration of its own laws. The supply of political influence is determined by the host country's political stability, the level of governmental competence, the discretion of the bureaucracy, and cultural or legal norms.

The authors recognize that corrupt practices are endemic throughout much of the world, but argue for their discontinuation on economic as much as legal/political grounds. They recommend the development of international codes of conduct to be followed by the multinationals, home governments and host governments. This recommendation addresses the demand, but not the supply side of corrupt practices.

Unless the factors prompting government officials to extort foreigners are resolved, multinationals will be unable to resist those demands. An international approach would reduce the competitive liability under which U.S.-based firms are currently operating.

Kapoor, Ashok and Philip D. Grub. ***The Multinational Enterprise in Transition: Selected Readings and Essays.*** **Princeton: The Darwin Press, 1972, p. 505.**

This is a collection of excellent essays by leading scholars in the field of international business. Articles are presented by Vernon, Dunning, Behrman, Hymer, Hirschman, Robinson, Stobaugh, Root, Harry Johnson, Fayerweather, Schollhammer, Aharoni, Jacoby and Robock. The collection puts the multinational enterprise in perspective by defining the problem, examining growth trends and reviewing measurement issues. Problems of corporate structure, organization and managment are also discussed at length. The key issue is the integration of foreign operations into a global corporate plan and the establishment of effective control over affiliates. One aspect of developing a genuinely international management team is to understand and adapt to local conditions abroad. Other topics include marketing, finance and accounting.

The challenge of economic nationalism is faced squarely. Political risks are discussed in terms of operational risk, transfer risk and operational control. Root defines the type of political analysis that should be done in support of corporate decision- making. "Political analysis is a method of inquiry that seeks to explain the political behavior of a host country and its consequences for the international enterprise. It goes beyond the 'What' of information to get at the 'Why' of change or stability, and it is directed towards the detection and measurement of causal factors and their mutual interdependence. A major tool of analysis is the model, a representation of reality in a conceptual form. A model identifies critical factors (variables), their mutual interdependence, and (given reliable information), the probable outcome of their interaction in specific circumstances."

Keohane, Robert O., and Joseph S. Nye, Jr. ***Power and Interdependence: World Politics in Transition.*** **Boston: Little, Brown and Company, 1977, p. 273.**

Keohane and Nye are dissatisfied with the realist approach to international political economy and develop an analytic framework to explain change at the international system level. Their model is applied to international regimes for oceans and money but could be easily transferred to foreign direct investment. An international regime is defined as the procedures, rule and institutions that shape behavior of key public and private actors in a given area.

The realist model assumes that states are unitary and rational actors and that states are the dominant actors in world affairs. It also assumes that force is a usable and effective instrument for policy. Finally, the realist perspective assumes that there is a definite hierarchy of issues in world politics ranging from the 'High' issues of strategic policy and diplomacy to the 'Low' issues of trade and finance. The authors offer an alternative to the realist perspective with their *complex interdependence* framework. This approach assumes multiple actors and channels of interaction, the blurring of high and low politics and the declining utility or relevance of force in international relations.

Keohane, Robert O., and Joseph S. Nye, Jr. (eds.) ***Transnational Relations and World Politics.*** **Cambridge, Mass: Harvard University Press, 1972, p. 428.**

This collection first appeared as a special issue of *International Organization* (Summer 1971). Transnational relations are defined in both their political and economic dimension. An overview of the growth of non-governmental international organizations (largely multinational corporations) in the twentieth- century is provided. A variety of transnational organizations are included: multinational corporations, foundations, religious organizations, and revolutionary groups. Functional concerns include the movement of funds internationally, air transportation and the organization of labor on an international basis. The contributors conclude that this last development is unlikely to meet with much success.

Kindleberger, Charles P. (ed.) *The International Corporation.* **Cambridge, Mass: MIT Press, 1970, p. 415.**

This collection reviews theories of foreign direct investment, the efficiency and welfare implications of multinational corporations, and the growth of non-American companies throughout the international economy. In terms of finance and technology, direct investment controls are reviewed as are effects of FDI on the balance of payments of investing and borrowing countries. The impact of U.S. investment on economic growth in Western Europe is also analyzed.

Political and legal factors are not ignored in this broad ranging study. The problem of national jurisdiction and the international firm is reviewed. The contributors argue that the host country remains dependent on foreign countries and firms for technology, organizational skills, and management expertise even after local subsidiaries have been nationalized. The contributors are not sanguine about the ability of host countries to unilaterally reverse their dependence on the international economic system.

Kindleberger, Charles P. ***American Business Abroad.*** **New Haven: Yale University Press, 1969, p. 225.**

These essays review theories of foreign investment, U.S. concerns with direct investment, patterns of U.S. direct investment in Western Europe and Japan, investments in developing countries, and the rise of the international corporation as an economic form.

Kudrle, Robert T., and Davis B. Bobrow. "U.S. Policy Toward Foreign Direct Investment." ***World Politics.*** **24(3), (April 1982): 353-79.**

The authors develop a framework to explain and forecast U.S. policy toward inward and outward foreign direct investment that will interpret stability and change and distinguish how policies are handled (e.g. with Presidential discretion, generated by Congress or because of public opinion). U.S. foreign policy is a function of U.S. domestic pressures, desires for national autonomy and national security considerations. The process of policymaking is characterized by ideological consonance, varying degrees of transparency of the impact of policies, perceptions of the diffusion or concentration of economic costs and benefits, and the political capacity of interest groups and political institutions.

Kumar, Krishna, and Maxwell G. McLeonard (eds). ***Multinationals from Developing Countries.*** **Lexington, Mass: D.C. Heath and Company, 1981, p. 211.**

This collection is based on a conference held at the East-West Center, University of Hawaii during 1979. Louis Wells presents information on the multinationalization of firms from developing countries. Approximately 1,100 firms have international operations. Most of this is in manufacturing (e.g. textiles, light assembly) with investment taking place in countries at a lower level of economic development than the home country. Third World leaders in this trend are India, South Korea, Taiwan, Hong Kong, Indonesia, and the major countries of Latin America. Dunning argues that multinationalization of Third World enterprises should be examined in the light of variables used to explain international expansion of firms from developed countries. These factors include but are not limited to the size and character of markets, level of resource endowments and government policies.

LaPalombara, Joseph, and Stephen Blank. ***Multinational Corporations in Comparative Perspective.*** **New York: The Conference Board, 1977, p. 76.**

This research study examines the environmental setting for international business. Key elements in this setting are host country attitudes toward business and specific regulations of the multinationals. The authors examine the role of expatriate and indigenous managers, local demands for equity participation, fiscal controls, national development aspirations, and investment strategies. Much attention is directed to the use of joint ventures with local private partners or the host government. Corporate attitudes towards joint ventures are described.

Several modes of country assessment were uncovered during this study of American multinationals. One of the most prevalent is the "Old Hands" or "Wise Men" approach. Using talent inside or outside of the firm, these approaches rely on people with great experience in international affairs (e.g. former Secretaries of State) or experts on particular countries. These last can be either American or indigenous experts. A second style is to use host country nationals of political or social prominence, or local information brokers as sources on political risk. Government agencies and officials of the parent countries as well as corporate external affairs departments are sources of information about local environments and operating conditions. In this short text, LaPalombara and Blank review sources of information for country assessment. As evidenced in later works, their general conclusion about country assessment is valid. Compared to economic analysis, political analysis in major companies is subjective, based on instinct or "feel" and is not based on systematic data or rigorous modeling methods.

Lipson, Charles. "Corporate Preferences and Public Policies: Foreign Aid Sanctions and Investment Protection." *World Politics.* **28(3), (April 1976): 396-421.**

Lipson tests alternative explanations of the policy process using bureaucratic, pluralist and radical perspectives. He reviews the sporadic application of the Hickenlooper and Gonzales Amendments. The latter prohibited U.S. approval of multilateral loans to countries that expropriated U.S. investors without paying "prompt, adequate and effective compensation". Lipson argues that changes in corporate preferences over time (desires for hard action mellowing) reflect the emergence of nationalist governments that were economically powerful. Overall, Lipson concludes, that U.S. policy reflected corporate preferences but not necessarily the preferences of corporations that had undergone divestment in the Third World.

McKern, Robert Bruce. *Multinational Enterprises and Natural Resources.* **Sydney, Australia: McGraw-Hill, 1976, p. 252.**

This study focuses on the minerals industry in Australia. The author presents an analytic framework for looking at investor and host country motivations and bargaining strengths in the area of natural resource investment. McKern examines the ownership position of foreigners in the following sectors of the Australian minerals industry: iron ore, black coal, lead, zinc, copper, petroleum, uranium, nickel, and aluminum. The financial resources of the foreign investor are discussed along with their technological advantages, management skills and marketing networks. Major minerals projects of the 1960s are reviewed.

Madden, Carl H. *The Case for the Multinational Corporation.* **New York: Praeger, 1971, p. 212**

This edited collection begins with the observation that multinationals accounted for 25 percent of world GNP in 1970 and that U.S. based firms were responsible for about half of that production. Madden argues that multinationals have effectively responded to the unequal distribution of human and physical resources and, by concentrating on factors of production rather than political boundaries, have made efficient use of global resources.

Specific articles are concerned with the ability of multinationals to overprice their goods (conclusion: they do not), the economic effects of multinationals on home and host countries, the effects of multinationals on U.S. economic independence and diversity, preferential U.S. tax treatment for companies doing business overseas, the power of multinationals in developing countries, and the impact of companies on national and international planning.

Megateli, Abderahmane. *Investment Policies of National Oil Companies: A Comparative Study of Sonatrach, NIOC and Pemex.* **New York: Praeger Publishers, 1980, p. 305.**

This study focuses on the investment policies and performance of three state-owned oil companies in the Third World: Algeria's Sonatrach; Iran's NIOC; and, Mexico's Pemex. The time period covered is the early 1970s. The author provides historical background on the development of each corporation, an examination of national petroleum policy objectives and principles, and an analysis of investment and planning with special emphasis on exploration. The study is based on personal interviews with company managers and government officials and publicly available statistical data.

Algeria's policy objectives were derived from a socialist perspective on development. National policy was directed against foreign domination of the industry and the direction by the state of economic development in partnership with labor. Iran's policies under the late Shah were based on the Petroleum Act of 1954 and aimed at an expansion of exploration and production and the inclusion of downstream activities in Iran. Spinoffs to other sectors of the economy were also desired. Mexico aimed at the integration of petroleum with the economy overall, the formation of domestic capital stock, an increase in petroleum production and reserves, and the use of petroleum based financial resources to stimulate regional and social development.

Modelski, George (ed.). *Multinational Corporations and World Order.* **Beverly Hills: Sage Publications, 1972, p. 160.**

Modelski presents an overview of the growth of multinational corporations and the military and industrial linkages of U.S.-based companies. Data on elite attitudes in Canada, France and the U.K. toward multinationals are presented. Although these elite surveys are dated at this point, they serve as a baseline against which to measure change in these three countries that are key or U.S. foreign investment.

Among the contributers, Robert Barnes presents a narrative on wealth deprivations of the international oil companies (Standard Oil of New Jersey and the Royal Dutch Shell Group) over the period 1918 to 1969. Based on company public records, 533 wealth deprivation events were recorded. Barnes concludes that, overall, wealth deprivation has had a minor effect on the health of these major oil companies. Barnes traces the strength of the oil majors in the face of numerous wealth deprivations to their domestic political power, their technical expertise, their organizational and managerial capabilities and their global integration.

Moran, Theodore H. "Foreign Expansion as an Institutional Necessity for U.S. Corporate Capitalism: The Search for a Radical Model." ***World Politics.*** **25(3), (April 1973): 369-86.**

Moran reviews alternative explanations of the international expansion of U.S. based companies. Explanations include surplus capital, declining profit rates, and reliance on sources of raw materials. The 'Institutional necessity' model is consistent with explanations based on the product cycle. Foreign direct investment follows trade in order to defend market share and find lower labor costs. Even on a small scale, FDI provides an option and hedge for the future. The 'necessity' of foreign investment can be understood at the level of the individual company whose managers seek to maintain flexibility in sourcing, plant location and marketing.

Negandhi, Anant R., and B. Rajaram Baliga. *Quest for Survival and Growth: A Comparative Study of American, European and Japanese Multinationals.* **New York: Praeger Publishers, 1977, p. 163.**

The authors examine the sources of conflict in corporate/government relations, the impact of managerial orientation and policies on these relations, the contribution of multinationals to the host economy, and prospects for controlling the multinational. They focus on six developing countries: Brazil, India, Malaysia, Peru, Singapore and Thailand. Interviews were conducted with 124 multinationals with subsidiaries in these countries to collect data on management style, sector, level of technology, subsidiary size, extent of diversification, relative market power of the multinational, the number of years in country and the market orientation (domestic or export) of the local subsidiary. Working with U.S. State Department documents and other public sources, Negandhi and Baliga catalogue 119 instances of conflict over foreign direct investment worldwide. The major sources of conflict were equity participation, indigenization of management and transfer pricing.

Negandhi, Anant R., and S. Benjamin Prasad. *The Frightening Angels: A Study of U.S. Multinationals in Developing Nations.* **Ohio: Kent State University Press, 1971, p. 249.**

This study examines the operations of U.S. multinationals in Argentina, Brazil, India, the Philippines and Uruguay. It compares management practices of U.S-based and local firms, examines the specific contributions of U.S. companies to technology transfer, and discusses current and likely future sources of tension. The study is based on data collected form 47 U.S.-owned subsidiaries and 45 comparable local firms. Interviews concentrated on management philosophy which was shown to affect strategic planning, leadership styles, motivations and policymaking.

Nye, Joseph S., Jr. "Multinational Corporations in World Politics." *Foreign Affairs.* **53(1) (October 1974): 153-75.**

Nye reports the rise to political prominence of the multinational corporation. He presents a qualified "No" to the obsolesence of the nation-state, however. The importance of the multinationals is increased because of the greater role that the social welfare function plays on the agenda of national governments. Multinationals often have a direct political role in host country life. They may also have an unintended direct role as instruments of influence of their home governments (e.g. the U.S. Trading with the Enemy Act). Multinationals' strongest role is in their indirect effects on national politics through their economic impact agenda setting function.

Ozawa, Terutomo. "Japan's Multinational Enterprise: The Political Economy of Outward Dependency. *World Politics.* **30(4), (July 1978): 517-37; and,** *Multinationalism, Japanese Style: The Political Economy of Outward Dependency.* **Princeton: Princeton University Press, 1979.**

Japan ranks fourth in total outward direct investment after the U.S., the U.K. and West Germany. Japan ranks first or second, however, in Brazil, Thailand, Indonesia, South Korea, Taiwan and Malaysia. Japan's outward expansion has been the result of national factors rather than firm specific characteristics. These national factors are the dependence of the Japanese economy on foreign markets for both exports and imports, rising environmental costs of industrial activity at home, and increasing costs for Japanese land and labor. Ozawa emphasizes the key role of trading companies in Japan's international investment and trade to third parties.

Olson, Richard Stuart. "Economic Coercion in World Politics: With a Focus on North-South Economic Relations." ***World Politics.*** **31(3), (July 1979): 471-94.**

This articles reviews the literature of international sanctions, dependency, and political instability. Olson argues that earlier studies understated the role of subtle forms of coercion because they focused on forms of coercion that were legislated (e.g. Hickenlooper) and highly public in their application. Highly public sanctions will more often fail because they stimulate nationalism and political integration in the target state. Moderate economic sanctions may be more politically effective because they exploit the *fragmented interest group and class structure* of developing countries. Properly applied, sanctions can cause relative deprivation which contributes to political instability in the target state.

Packenham, Robert A. *Liberal America and the Third World.* **Princeton: Princeton University Press, 1973, p. 395.**

Packenham reviews the state of political development doctrines in two periods of American foreign policy: 1947-60 and 1961-68. He examines the liberal roots of these doctrines, their relationship to thinking about economic development and academic theories of political change. The theme of this book is the relationship between views in the United States Government about democratic development and the foreign aid program.

Penrose, Edith T. *The Large International Firm in Developing Countries: The International Petroleum Industry.* **London: George Allen and Unwin, Ltd., 1968, p. 311.**

Penrose focuses on the economics of the institution (the international firm) through which foreign direct investment is made. Effects on home and host countries are not directly considered in this classic study. Penrose reviews the nature and significance of the large international firm in terms of its vertical integration, nationality, and the financial role of stockholders. The historical development of the petroleum industry is presented. Individual petroleum companies are analyzed. The control of supply by the international petroleum companies is also presented. The role of these companies in developing countries is reviewed. Sources of conflict with governments include financial problems (profits, taxation) and local resentment of the economic and political power of the corporation.

Purdie, William, K., and Bernard Taylor (eds.). *Business Strategies for Survival: Planning for Social and Political Change.* **London: Heineman, 1976, p. 231.**

Changing social values are affecting the ways businesses must plan their future operations. Major social changes are taking place with regard to the role of women, business' responsibility to consumers, protection of the environment, and the expansion in the number of immigrant workers. Keyed to British industry, Purdie, Taylor and their collaborators argue for increased social responsibility and political activism. Contrary to the advice given to foreign firms by most authors, these analysts advise British companies to play a direct role in local and national political life.

Robinson, Richard D. *International Business Managment: A Guide to Decision Making.* **Hinsdale, Illinois: The Dryden Press, 1978, p. 686.**

This business text begins with a consideration of the role of business in a nationalistic world. Sources of local pressure on the international firm are described. Effects of international business on world welfare are also reviewed. Strategies for the management of sales, supply, labor, ownership, finance and affiliate control are presented.

Robock, Stefan, and Kenneth Simmonds. *International Business and Multinational Enterprises.* **Homewood, Illinois: Richard D. Irwin, 1983, p. 772.**

Robock and Simmonds in their third edition of this standard business text, define international business, describe its patterns and review theories of international business expansion. Specific topics reviewed include foreign exchange and international money markets, the international monetary system, balance of payments, international trade flows and trade institutions, international law and investment dispute settlement machinery. Special attention is directed to the impact of the nation-state on international business. National controls, the variety of political risks, and the countervailing power of the foreign firm are reviewed. In the section on building a global strategy, Robock and Simmonds include material on economic and demand assessment and political risk analysis. Traditional topics are also well covered: management, accounting, technology transfer and marketing. Five cases are presented on multinational management.

Rolfe, Sidney E., and Walter Damm (eds.). *The Multinational Corporation in the World Economy.* **New York: Prager Publishers, 1970, p. 169.**

This collection of original articles is based on a conference held in 1969 under the auspices of the Atlantic Institute, the Atlantic Council of the United States and the Committee for Atlantic Cooperation. Contributors review the development of the international corporation, economic aspects of West European investment in the United States, the legal aspects of that investment, U.S. anti-trust policy towards outward foreign investment, and the activities of U.S. based investors in Canada and Western Europe.

Rosen, Steven J., and James R. Kurth (eds.). *Testing Theories of Economic Imperialism.* **Lexington, Mass: D.C. Heath and Company, 1974, p. 284.**

Rosen and Kurth present a collection of original articles on theories of imperialism and neo- imperialism and empirical or quantitative tests of those theories. Theoretical overviews of new forms of imperialism and the role of the multinational corporation are provided by Kurth, Karl W. Deutsch, Andrew Mack, Thomas E. Weisskopf and Harry Magdoff. James Caporaso reviews methodological issues involved in the measuring inequality, dependence and exploitation - key concepts in the academic literature on imperialism. Testing of these approaches is provided by John S. Odell (U.S. military aid), Theodore H. Moran (large resource investments and exploitation), Stephen D. Krasner (raw materials trade), and Walter Goldstein (U.S. economic penetration of Western Europe. Two articles on Soviet imperialism are also included.

Sampson, Anthony. ***The Seven Sisters: The Great Oil Companies and the World They Shaped.*** **New York: Viking Press, 1975, p. 334.**

This popular study focuses on the historical development of the seven major companies that have dominated the oil industry since its beginnings in the late nineteenth-century. Their influence remains pervasive today, despite a major shift in power that took place with the embargo and price hike in 1973–74 initiated by the Organization of Petroleum Exporting Countries (OPEC). The Seven Sisters are based in the United States (Exxon, Mobil, Texaco, Socal and Gulf), the United Kingdom (BP), and the Netherlands (Shell). They are, however, genuinely international in the scope of their activities.

Sampson's central question is "Who Controls?" For almost a century world oil production was controlled by major companies from the leading market economies. Operating as a *de facto* if not a *de jure* cartel, the majors set production levels, determined prices, allocated market share, integrated across the entire range of petroleum activities, and, in many instances, assumed major diplomatic or political functions. The operation of this cartel, most blatant during the heyday of the Standard Oil Company of New Jersey (now Exxon), continued virtually uninhibited until the early 1950s.

The effectiveness of this private cartel in controlling the world petroleum market was undermined after World War II by several factors. These included the burgeoning demand for gasoline caused by the motorization of the West, the discovery of vast reserves in the Middle East, and the growth of independents that acquired footholds in some of the new territories. The private cartel's existence was successfully challenged by the formation and development of OPEC. Beginning in 1973, OPEC assumed the pricing and production functions formerly exercised by the sisters. By their success in bringing modern education and industrial methods to the developing countries, the multinational oil companies made possible their own displacement by national governments committed to sovereign control over their own resources.

Sampson, Anthony. *The Money Lenders: Bankers in a Dangerous World.* **London: Coronet Books, 1981, p. 377.**

The major themes of this narrative history of international banking are the role of individuals in shaping organizations, institutions and decision-making, and the factors that effect the risk of default and creditworthiness across time and countries. Major developments in the twentieth-century covered by Sampson include the interrelationship of U.S. political and economic hegemony, the shift of banking from the U.K. to the U.S., and the growth in Eurodollars.

The current high level of attention focused on the creditworthiness of the developing countries has historical parallels. The similarity of the Third World's financial condition to that of England in the fourteenth-century (vis-a-vis Italian bankers) and that of the United States in the nineteenth-century (vis-a-vis British creditors) is often overlooked by today's creditor nations. Sampson devotes a chapter to the problem of country risk assessment. He reviews the cases of Brazil, Turkey and Poland, castigates the bankers for their herd mentality, and notes institutional tensions within banks (loan vs. credit officers) that may inhibit impartial country assessment.

Stephenson, Hugh. *The Coming Clash: The Impact of Multinational Companies on Nation-States.* **New York: Saturday Review Press, 1972, p. 185**

Stephenson joins the chorus of the early 1970s in announcing the demise of the nation- state. Sovereignty has been undermined by the growth of the multinational corporation and the replacement of portfolio with direct foreign investment. In a new industrial revolution, international trade was replaced in the 1950s and 1960s by investment as the primary vehicle of international exchange. The response of national governments to the power of the multinational corporation has been anemic. Stephenson comments that "(n)ationalist reaction to the march of the international leviathan has often been muddled or illogical." (p. 87). Countervailing power has also been inadequate. Writing in the early 1970s for a 1972 publication, Stephenson argued that cartels had been effective (true) and that labor unions had been slow to organize on an international basis to solve problems posed by the multinational corporation (also true). However, as suggested by Stephenson's title, conflict between the multinational and the nation-state was coming. Nationalization of foreign investments by Third World governments peaked in the four years following publication of *The Coming Clash.*

Sunkel, Osvaldo. "Big Business and 'Dependencia', A Latin American View." ***Foreign Affairs.*** **50 (April 1972): 517-31.**

Writing about the same time as Stephenson (see previous entry), Sunkel comes to a radically different conclusion about the future of government-business relations in the Third World. For Sunkel, the winds of nationalism were blowing strong. In Latin America leftist governments were in place in Chile, Peru and Bolivia. Nationalizations of foreign investment were occuring with greater frequency and restrictive investment regulations were in force in the Andean Common Market Countries. This rising nationalism in Latin America was due to changes in the internal social, economic and political structure, according to Sunkel. Sunkel described the process by which multinational corporations penetrate the political and economic life of the host country, dominant its economy and finances, and undercut the economic and political base of the national bourgeoisie.

Tanzer, Michael. *The Political Economy of International Oil and the Underdeveloped Countries.* **Boston: Beacon Press, 1969, p. 435.**

A Harvard-trained economist, Tanzer worked for Esso Standard Eastern. His formal academic training and experience excellently equip him for this study that contains an intellectual debt to Harry Magdoff. Tanzer focuses on the impact of oil on the oil-importing LDCs, their requirement for energy and the high cost (in 1969!) of imported oil. Tanzer reviews the basic economics of the international oil industry and describes the activities of the major players: the Seven Sisters, governments of producing and consuming countries and state-owned oil companies. In an unfortunately short-sighted prediction, Tanzer argued that nationalization was unlikely in the international oil industry. Would be nationalizers are deterred by (1) existence of alternative sellers in the international market; (2) the isolation of the oil sector in producing countries; and, (3) the dependence of oil exporters on the industrial nations for political support.

Turner, Louis. *Oil Companies in the International System.* **London: George Allen and Unwin, second edition, 1980, p. 254.**

Turner characterizes the oil companies as new actors in world politics that blur traditional distinctions between the "high politics" of diplomacy and strategy and the low politics of trade and finance. Turner reviews the historical development of the international industry from the end of World War II and discusses a long series of conflicts between the companies and host governments in the Third World. Although governments control access, corporate strengths lie in their financial resources, technology for exploration and development, and their ownership or access to transportation and marketing networks. The 1970s brought the end of the concession system, an increase in the earnings of producer states and the loss of control by multinationals over pricing and production decisions.

Turner, Louis. *Multinational Corporations and the Third World.* **New York: Hill and Wang, 1973, p. 294.**

Turner discusses the political, economic and social aspects of clashes and confrontations between multinationals and Third World governments. The book is based on journalistic sources, interviews and published documents. It chronicles the rising assertiveness of the Third World during the 1960s and 1970s. Turner assesses the effects of economic domination on local entrepreneurship, government finance, and the balance of payments. A chapter is devoted to sources of economic nationalism (pp. 74–112) which are defined as ideology, growth in information (the learning curve), and Third World institutions (Group of 77, OPEC, UN, ECLA, etc.). Demands of economic nationalists have increased from boosting financial returns (royalties, taxes), to regulating the multinational's impact on the host economy, to local equity participation.

United Nations, Centre on Transnational Corporations. *Transnational Corporations in World Development: A Re-Examination.* **New York: United Nations, 1978, p. 343.**

Trends in policies toward transnational corporations are examined in the context of increasing awareness of the effects of these companies on national development. Recognizing that the global strategy of transnationals may conflict with national objectives, many host countries have used nationalization to achieve such goals as local control, technology transfer and a greater role for nationals in their country's economic life. Transnationals continue to grown in their international influence; transnationals are more diverse with new companies emerging from leading Third World countries; transnationals continue to focus most of their activities in the developed market economies. Eighty-nine statistical tables are presented on transnational activities and extent of nationalization during the 1960s and 1970s.

United Nations, Centre on Transnational Corporations. *Multinational Corporations in World Development.* **New York: Praeger Publishers, 1974, p. 200.**

This study reviews existing policies toward multinational corporations and proposes national, regional and international courses of action. Substantial appendices include information on relevant U.N. Resolutions and statistical data on transnational companies. The transnational corporation is defined and its activities are described by sector and geographic region. Sources of tension with the host country are reviewed. These include threats to national sovereignty, conflicts with national development objectives, transfers of technology and skills, labor relations, balance of payments effects and taxation.

United States, Department of State. *Factors Influencing the Pattern of Private Foreign Direct Investment Among LDCs.* **Washington, D.C: Bureau of Intelligence and Research, October 1973, p. 13.**

This study examines foreign direct investment flows from Development Assistance Countries to 36 LDCs between 1968 and 1971. Growth of foreign direct investment is a function of the initial level of investment (a proxy measure for the overall business climate), GNP growth and imports growth (measures of market size). Investment flows are correlated positively with Western economic aid, negatively with Soviet bloc aid, and negatively with host country expropriations of U.S. and other foreign investment. This study found no general effect of taxation and tariff policies on overall investment flows.

Vernon, Raymond. *The Economic and Political Consequences of Multinational Enterprise: An Anthology.* **Boston: Harvard University Graduate School of Business Administration, 1972, p. 236.**

The themes of this collection are technological change and a shrinking world, the relationship between U.S. hegemony and the expansion of U.S. firms, and the use of overseas investment as a tool to protect market share by U.S. companies. Specific topics include *sovereignty at bay*, choices facing developing countries between foreign trade and foreign investment, the tension between multinational enterprise freedoms and national security for both home and host countries, and the future of the multinational enterprise.

Vernon, Raymond. "Multinationals: No Strings Attached." *Foreign Policy.* **33 (Winter 1978-79): 121-34.**

Vernon reviews the inconsistent nature of U.S. policy toward outward foreign direct investment. The foreign investor is Janus-like: a citizen of the host country, he also is subject to the laws and policies of the United States. Much of the inconsistency in U.S. policy toward the foreign investor results from the absence of a national investment policy. Investment policy is the indirect result of policies aimed at Third World development, U.S. balance of payments corrections, and U.S. employment objectives. While the U.S. government generally supports increased foreign investment, it has historically looked the other way when the chips were down. The absence of effective investment protection results from the complex nature of U.S. interests around the world and the existence of hostages (remaining investments) in nationalizing countries.

Vernon, Raymond. *Sovereignty at Bay.* New York: Basic Books, 1971, p. 326.

This is the classic argument from liberal political-economy about the spread of multinational enterprise throughout the world. Based on data from the Harvard Multinational Enterprise Project, Vernon advances the product cycle model as the explanation for this multinational expansion and the obsolescing bargain model as the best explanatory theory of host country - investor interaction. Vernon argues correctly and presciently that the real issue is not tax policy or overlapping national jurisdiction but local control. The stumbling block in host country - enterprise relations will be effective control over the basic production, employment, pricing and marketing (exporting) decisions of the firm. In certain industries, particularly in resource extraction, these factors are critical to national welfare. Using extensive data Vernon reviews the economic effects of multinational enterprise on national economic performance of both the advanced economies and the developing nations.

Vernon, Raymond. "Sovereignty at Bay After Ten Years." *International Organization.* 35(3), (Summer 1981): 517-30.

Vernon takes a hard look back at *Sovereignty at Bay* in the light of numerous criticisms of the work and subsequent events in the developing world (OPEC and extensive nationalizations) that offered evidence that it was the multinational enterprise, not the nation-state, that was at bay. Vernon argued, with some reason, that the erosion of the oligopoly power of the multinational was foreseen in *Sovereignty at Bay*. The growth of national capabilities, the entrance of new firms into the extractive industries, the expansion of manufacturing firms from other advanced states and the newly industrializing countries was anticipated in the earlier analysis of the obsolescing bargain model. Vernon admits that the choice of the title biased his audience away from the factors that could lead to an erosion of the influence of the multinational. Despite these arguments from hindsight, Vernon's earlier work was pathbreaking and influential in the cogency of his arguments about the internationalization of business enterprises.

Vernon, Raymond. ***Storm Over the Multinationals: The Real Issues.*** **Cambridge: Harvard University Press, 1977, p. 260; and "Storm Over the Multinationals: Problems and Prospects."** ***Foreign Affairs.*** **55(2), (January 1977): 243-62.**

Vernon focuses on the manufacturing enterprise as the best symbol of an interdependent world. Working within the perspective of liberal political economy, Vernon argues that technology is the driving international force determining preferences among consumers and shaping the opportunities for multinationals. Vernon characterizes the multinational enterprise by its size, degree of multinationality, and national base (increasing number of multinationals are from the Third World itself). The multinational is engaged in a drive for stability in the increasing competition between firms from the industrial states, the developing countries and state-owned enterprises from capitalist and socialist states.

Vernon, Raymond, and Louis T. Wells, Jr. *Economic Environment of International Business.* **Englewood Cliffs, N.J: Prentice-Hall, 1972, p. 246.**

Vernon and Wells review the strategies and structures of firms engaged in international operations. The multinational enterprise is viewed as a system of national production units. International currency transactions are assessed. National evaluation of enterprise contribution, conflicts with national institutions (businesses, labor unions, government agencies) are an unavoidable element in the firm's environment.

Waddams, Frank. *The Libyan Oil Industry.* **Baltimore: Johns Hopkins University Press, 1980, p. 331.**

Waddams provides a historical and chronological analysis of the development of the Libyan oil industry. Key events are the Libyan Petroleum Law of 1955, amendments to that law in 1961, a new petroleum law in 1965, and the overthrow of the monarchy in 1969. Although Qhadaffi has received much attention for asserting national control over foreign enterprises, this process began earlier under Idris II. Waddams' study has value for the beginning student of the oil industry as well as the Libyan specialist. He reviews the technical aspects of exploration and production, the financial aspects (profits, taxation, royalties), the international legal context, and the growth of competition from the independents. For the Libyan specialist, he provides an analysis of the impact of the oil industry on the national economy, Libya's role in OPEC and the development of Libya's national oil company.

Wells, Louis T., Jr. ***Third World Multinationals: The Rise of Foreign Investment from Developing Countries.*** **Cambridge, Mass: MIT Press, 1983, p. 206.**

The expansion of foreign direct investment from Third World states is attributed to increasing protectionism against exports and contractual problems with licensing arrangements. Wells' conclusions are based on personal interviews and data on the incorporation and operation of subsidiaries of 963 parent Third World companies established in 125 developing countries. Third World companies possess certain competitive advantages derived from experience in their home markets. These include use of small-scale production processes, locally available inputs and the production of items appropriate to Third World markets. However, these advantages are only temporary as there are no barriers to local firms developing such skills. Practices associated with foreign investment from developed economies are not followed -- by choice or necessity -- by Third World investors. Third World manufacturing firms have low research and development expenditures, little trade name loyalty or product differentiation, and seldom establish integrated production facilities across several countries that would achieve efficient plant size and hedge vulnerability to political risk.

Yoshino, M.Y. ***Japan's Multinational Enterprises.*** **Cambridge: Harvard University Press, 1976, p. 191.**

The international expansion of Japan's multinationals followed the erosion of their traditional strategy of market penetration through exports. This strategy eroded because of import restrictions, the changing content of Japan's exports, a decline in the enterprises' ability to protect their domestic market and secure raw materials, and the decline of Japan's status as a low-cost producer. The outward expansion of Japanese manufacturing firms is particularly noteworthy. In fields as diverse as auto manufacturing and synthetic fibers, Japanese have concentrated on investing in the developing countries (sources of raw materials and cheap labor). Seventy percent of Japanese outward foreign direct investment is in developing countries with sixty percent in Asia. Following the example of the major trading companies, multinational enterprises are expanding ito third country trade as well as exporting back to Japan.

Yoshino argues that traditional Japanese management practices (Ringi) are a constraint on foreign operations and that they are unlikely to converge with U.S. practices. The Ringi system is based on management by consensus and relies on shared values and experiences. With a growing number of Japanese managers overseas, decision-making is inevitably slowed. Pressures in the host country for indigenization of management at the local level will erode the cultural basis for management - Japanese style.

Chapter Three: Sources of Political Risk

Akinsanya, Adeoye A. *The Expropriation of Multinational Property in the Third World.* **New York: Praeger Publishers, 1980, p. 386.**

This comparative study focuses on the expropriation policies of selected developing countries: Chile, Cuba, Egypt, Guyana, Indonesia, Iran, Libya, Sri Lanka, Tanzania and Zambia. Foreign subsidiaries in all major economic sectors have been expropriated in one or more of these countries. Expropriations of firms in natural resource extraction and agriculture have been most prevalent.

Expropriations between 1950 and 1978 are analyzed on the basis of corporate documents, government reports and press reports. Narrative accounts discuss the qualitative factors that caused economic nationalism in these nations. Although the author often demonstrates an ideological bias in the choice of wording and a tendency to blame the companies for their own expropriation, a mix of motives for expropriation are presented and analyzed. Nationalism, desires for economic sovereignty, demands for increased economic benefits from foreign activity, and prospects for political benefit to the nationalizing government are all documented as causes of expropriation. A major weakness of this study is its omission of much useful quantitative data relevant to the testing of hypotheses raised in the narrative.

Expropriation and other forms of political risk are defined, international legal norms relating to the treatment of foreign investment are presented, each expropriation or nationalization is detailed, and an extensive set of references is provided.

Apter, David E. "Nationalism, Government Change and Economic Growth." *Economic Development and Cultural Change.* **7 (January 1959): 117-36.**

Apter focuses on the political demands facing the leaders of the developing nations. These demands, if anything, are more intense today. These leaders need to reconcile the widespread political participation required for legitimate government with the strong and stable leadership required for economic development. In a reversal of the classic economic development brings political development, a threshhold of political development must be crossed in order for economic modernization to occur. Sources of high expectations are reviewed. Key governmental functions are discussed. Elements of governmental viability include (1) accountability and consent, (2) authoritative decision-making, (3) political recruitment and role assignment, (4) resource and reserve allocation, and (5) coercion.

The most viable developing political system will be based on a fraternal, open, mass, congress-type party. Such a political system derives its legitimacy from its large support base and structures social mobility opportunities through party membership. Such systems tend to have a socialist ideology, tolerate a nominal opposition, and are pragmatic in their actions.

Avery, William P. "Innovation in Latin American Regionalism." *International Organization.* **27 (Spring 1973): 181-223.**

The Andean Common Market (ANCOM) was formed by Chile, Columbia, Ecuador, Peru, and Venezuela to offset the power of Argentina, Brazil, and Mexico and compensate for the slow progress of the Latin American Free Trade Association (LAFTA). ANCOM differs from LAFTA and the Central American Common Market in its higher level of integration, the common policy on foreign investment, regional planning for industry and agriculture and its quasi–supranational secretariat. Other factors contributing to regional integration include what Avery and Cochrane term elite complementarity (p. 219), shared external dependence, and similar domestic political systems.

Baklanoff, Eric N. *Expropriation of U.S. Investments in Cuba, Mexico and Chile.* **New York: Praeger Publishers, 1975, p. 170.**

There have been several key issues in U.S. - Latin American relations during the 1960s and 1970s. These are the Panama Canal, the 200 mile limit, economic aid, diplomatic recognition of Cuba, and the expropriation of U.S. investments. Baklanoff attributes expropriation in the three countries under study to "fundamental shifts in ideology and internal power coalitions." (vii). He compares the expropriation actions of Mexico (1936–38), Cuba (1959–60) and Chile (1971–73) and looks at their effect on MNC operations and U.S. investment policy. The role of ideology, asset valuation, legality of the nationalizations, and economic sanctions are examined for each investment dispute.

Bates, Robert H. *Unions, Parties and Political Development: A Study of Mine Workers in Zambia.* **New Haven: Yale University Press, 1971, p. 291.**

Given the commitment of national elites to rapid economic development, Bates examines the nature of trade unions in developing countries, the relationship of labor to development, government labor policy in Zambia, the failure of that policy, and the role of the union in the growth of the mining industry. He focuses on the ability of the government to set social goals and regulate the political and economic behavior of groups to achieve those objectives.

Behrman, Jack N. "Multinational Corporations, Transnational Interests and National Sovereignty." ***Columbia Journal of World Business.*** **4 (March 1969): 30-36.**

Behrman examines sources of conflict between host governments and multinational corporations. These potential conflict areas include the right of intervention, the limits of state and enterprise authority, the responsibilities of management to shareholders, employees, customers and suppliers, and the direction of the allegiance of multinational companies. Perceptions in developing countries of loyalty to home governments or parent companies, while understandable, undermine local control.

Behrman, Jack N., J.J. Boddewyn, and Ashok Kapoor. ***International Business–Government Comunications: Structures, Actors and Issues.*** **Lexington, Mass: Lexington Books, 1975, p. 205.**

Key issues in this study are interdependence, legitimacy, and mutual adjustment. The authors review corporate structures and processes as they affect the government relations function. Political risk assessment is often conducted within the organizational context of government relations. The strategy adopted is a function of the firm's market orientation, industry, and patterns of ownership and managerial control. An element in any public or government relations strategy is the intelligence function (pp. 45–68). Information is distinguished from intelligence. Intelligence is collected, processed, evaluated, combined with other information available to the firm and, ideally, used as one element in the capital-budgeting process. Reporting structures, loci and criteria of assessment and analytic techniques are reviewed.

Bennett, Douglas C., and Kenneth E. Sharpe. "Agenda Setting and Bargaining Power: The Mexican State versus Transnational Automobile Corporations." ***World Politics.*** **32(1) (October 1979): 57-89.**

Bennett and Sharpe are concerned with agenda setting in relations between multinational corporations and host country governments. Specifically, agenda setting is the process by which issues come to the fore and become objects of conflict and bargaining. To explore their hypotheses about agenda setting, the authors use the case of the Mexican automobile industry as it developed between 1960 and 1964. Their research is based on personal interviews with executives in the Mexican automobile industry and government officials.

The development of the automobile industry in Mexico was the result of global market forces as well as local conditions and government objectives. Historically, the automobile industry had become increasingly concentrated. In 1973 eight firms accounted for 85 percent of production worldwide. This concentration was due, primarily, to economies of scale that favored long production runs. This benefitted producers that operated in or had access to large markets. The increasing concentration of the industry spurred competition even for small domestic markets like Mexico's.

Agenda setting is determined by several factors including the structure of the industry, the behavior of the firm and ownership of the firms. Unlike natural resources, state power vis-a-vis foreign manufacturing investors is greatest at the outset. Once the state has granted local market access to the multinational and it becomes integrated with the economy (suppliers, supplemental investment, labor) the power of the state declines. In response to this changing balance of power, the Mexican state has promoted indigenization of foreign direct investment but also has provided incentives for private investment and the political control of labor.

Bennett, Douglas and Kenneth E. Sharpe. "The State as Banker and Entrepreneur: The Last Resort Character of the Mexican State's Economic Intervention, 1917-76." ***Comparative Politics.*** **12(2) (January 1980): 165-89.**

Following the revolution, the Mexican state took the role of making capitalism work for Mexico. Because of the dependent condition of the country and the lateness of its industrialization, the Mexican state had to curtail the desires for consumption of the mass of the population and move into areas where the private sector would not or could not invest. These sectors included steel, paper, cement, the railroads, automobile manufacturing, banking and sugar.

The independence of the state was limited by two factors. Although foreign borrowing eased short-term dependence on domestic interests, it brought dependence in the long-term on foreign lenders. In recent years, the activism of the state has met increasing resistance from the national bourgeoisie that it helped create.

Bennett, Peter D., and Robert Green. "Political Instability as a Determinant of Direct Foreign Marketing Investment." ***Journal of Marketing Research.*** **9 (May 1972): 182-86; and, Green,** ***Political Instability as a Determinant of U.S. Foreign Investment*** **Austin: University of Texas, Bureau of Business Research, 1972, p. 122.**

Bennett and Green examine the relationship between political instability, market factors, and the distribution of flows of foreign direct investment in manufacturing across host countries worldwide.The approch is cross-national, quantitative and comparative. They hypothesize that political instability reduces the flow of foreign direct manufacturing investment, that this effect is greater in developing countries, that the effect is weaker in Latin America than other developing countries, that the annual flow of foreign investment is affected more by short- term rather than long-term political instability, and that a nation's long-term future is more a function of its own long-term past (in)stability than its recent performance. Overall, the statistical analyses did not support these hypotheses.

Berger, Peter L. *Pyramids of Sacrifice*. New York: Basic Books, 1974, p. 242.

Berger has presented an analysis of Third World development and political ethics as applied to problems of social change in developing countries. The book's metaphor is the sacrificial pyramid of Cholula, located in the Mexican state of Puebla. The pyramid is a stone structure, dedicated to a set of theories about politics, social life and ethics. It was built by the labor of countless peasants and sustained by their blood sacrifices. It is not dissimilar to current pyramids of capitalism and socialism. Berger debunks both capitalism and socialism with equal rigor and fervor. Arguing for more participation by the common man, he advocates more humane approaches to political and economic development. Overall, the book provides insight into sources of political dissatisfaction and change in the Third World.

Bergner, D. J. "Political Risk Analysis: An Asset Now, Soon a Must". *Public Relations Quarterly*. 27(2) (Summer 1982): 28-31.

Political risk analysis has been a growing field since the mid-1970s. Much of this growth is due to events in the Third World (Iranian Revolution, war in Central America) that have seriously effected business operations. Other elements of political risk include general social developments and changes in host government policy. Both political and social risk analysis are recommended in addition to customary analyses of technical, economic and financial risk. Not only These new forms of risk complicate the tasks of corporate planners. Non-economic forms of risk are difficult to predict. This is due to the large number of factors that need to be considered in any evaluation of risk and the lack of a track record in most firms or consulting organizations of risk predictions.

Binder, Leonard, et al. *Crises and Sequences in Political Development.* **Princeton: Princeton University Press, 1971, p. 326.**

The contributers to this edited collection discuss the transition of organized societies from traditional structures to modern ones. Traditional societies are characterized by ascriptive norms for recognition, authority and reward, are particularistic in loyalties and diffuse in structure and hierarchy. Modern societies are achievement oriented, are universal in their application of norms or laws, and are functionally specific. The transition from traditional to modern is marked by several crises. These are the crises of identity, legitimacy, participation, penetration and distribution. Political development is affected by the sequence in which these crises occur and the extent to which they are sequential or concurrent.

Blake, David.H., and Robert E. Driscoll. *The Social and Economic Impacts of Transnational Corporations: Case Studies of U.S. Paper*

Industry in Brazil. **New York: Fund for Multinational Management Education, 1977, p. 133.**

The authors present a mixed qualitative and quantitative method for evaluating the impact of foreign investment on the development of the host country. Social, political, economic and human impacts are analyzed. The specific firms examined are Olinkraft, Ltda., and Rigera Celulose, Papel e Embalagems, Ltda. Variables included in the analysis are balance of payments effects, domestic expenditures, technology transfers, employment effects, voluntary and charitable activities, and local perceptions of impact.

Boarman, Patrick H., and Hans Schollhammer (eds.). *Multinational Corporations and Governments: Business- Government Relations in an International Context.* **New York: Praeger Publishers, 1975, p. 234.**

This edited collection is based on a conference held in the Fall of 1973 on "Multinational Corporations and Governments" under the auspices of the Center for International Business at Pepperdine University and the University of California at Los Angeles. The several articles cover the policies of the U.S. and Canada toward multinational corporations, a review of the Overseas Private Investment Corporation, an assessment of the effects of multinational corporations on international trade and an empirical comparison by Negandhi of multinational affiliates and local companies in Argentina, Brazil, India, the Philippines, Taiwan and Uruguay.

Neil Jacoby charts the growth of friction over time between multinationals and governments and calls for an international agency to enforce a code of conduct. Stefan Robock argued, conversely, that responsiblity for the behavior of the multinational lay with the home government, rather than the host government or an international agency. Boarman offered a word of caution that is as applicable in the 1980s as it was during the original conference. He argued against penalizing multinationals for the failure of governments (home and host) to solve their national monetary problems.

A key article is the piece by J.J. Boddewyn on six principles for effective government relations strategy. These are (1) government relations are unavoidable and important; (2) government relations are an earning function (not a cost center) for the firm; (3) government relations must be managed; they will not take care of themselves; (4) this management must take place at the top; (5) government relations are a legitimate function for senior managers; and, (6) effectively managed government relations can be mutually beneficial.

Bornschier, Volker, and Christopher Chase-Dunn. "Cross-National Evidence of the Effects of Foreign Investment and Aid on Economic Growth and Inequality: A Survey of Findings and a Re- Analysis." *American Journal of Sociology.* **84(3) (November 1978): 651-83.**

Bornschier and Chase-Dunn present a review of the quantitative literature and their own analysis of the effects of multinational corporations in their role as foreign investors on the economic growth and distributional equality of developing countries. Their analysis includes 76 developing countries worldwide over the period 1960-75. Using multiple regression techniques they test for the effects of foreign investment on the rate of growth of GNP per capita between 1960 and 1976 and changes in the sectoral distribution of income over the same period. Individual or household level data on income inequality would be germane; these are simply not available in a reliable and comprehensive manner.

The effects of foreign investment are divided into short- and long-term consequences. In the short-term, foreign direct investment increases the rate of GNP growth per capita. Over the longer-term, countries which have a high level of dependence on foreign investment and aid experience depressed levels of growth. These findings hold regardless of the regional location of the country. They might be altered through the use of more recent data that would capture more positive growth effects of foreign investment. The Newly Industrializing Countries (Taiwan, South Korea, Singapore, Brazil and Mexico) boast both high rates of growth and very high levels of foreign direct investment. The selection of the 1975 endpoint (appropriate when Bornschier and Chase-Dunn were writing) may bias the impact of foreign invesment downward.

Bosson, Rex and Bension Varon. ***The Mining Industry and the Developing Countries.*** **New York: Oxford University Press, 1977, p. 292.**

Bosson and Varon review the nature and structure of the mining industry, and assess mineral reserves and resources, production, processing, consumption and trade, and examine mineral price behavior. They analyze problems of mineral development in LDCs and review the objectives and policy tools of mineral sector development programs (pp. 151-77).

Bostock, Mark and Charles Harvey (eds.). ***Economic Independence and Zambian Copper: A Case Study of Foreign Investment.*** **New York: Praeger Publishers, 1972, p. 275.**

On August 11, 1969, President Kenneth Kaunda of Zambia offered Anglo-American and Roan Selection Trust the opportunity to sell 51 percent of their equity to the government of Zambia. This began the process that led to full nationalization during the early 1970s. Zambia was an example of extreme economic dependence. The foreign-owned copper industry accounted for 40 percent of GDP, 93 percent of export earnings, 68 percent of government revenues, and 15 percent of employment. Bostock and Harvey review the history of the copper industry, the nature of the traditional concession and the growth of pressures for local control.

Sources of conflict were identified as discrimination against locals in employment, training, and promotions; outflow of profits; insufficient reinvestment of earnings; decisions of the multinationals that worked against local development objectives; and suspicions of transfer pricing policies of the copper companies.

Boulton, Adam. "Jamaica's Bauxite Strategy: The Caribbean Flirts with the International System." ***SAIS Review.*** **(Summer 1981): 81-91.**

This narrative analysis focuses on the policies of the Manley government toward the international aluminum companies beginning with the formation of the International Bauxite Association in 1974. The author assesses the reasons for the admitted failure of Manley's policies. Boulton attributes this failure to the structure of the international bauxite industry rather than to the leftist policies of the Manley government. It is certainly the case that the concentration of the world bauxite industry and the availability of alternative supplies limited the power of the cartel. It is unfortunate for Jamaica that these factors were not foreseen.

Breton, Albert. "The Economics of Nationalism." *Journal of Political Economy.* **72 (August 1964): 376-86.**

Breton defines nationalism as an investment of resources in nationality or ethnicity. These investments (diversion of material resources) are made because they are profitable in a material or psychic sense. However, they are seldom equally profitable for everyone in society. Nationalism generates demands for an international or inter-ethnic transfer of opportunities and resources.

Nationalization or expropriation of foreign investors is one means for satisfying the demand for nationalism, at least in the short-term. Nationalization provides increased jobs, especially managerial jobs, for nationals. Depending on the form and amount of compensation, nationalization redirects the flow of earnings to nationals or the host country state itself. The economics of nationalism are rational from the point of view of group welfare, social status or political power. Such acts are seldom rational from the point of view of national economic welfare.

Bronfenbrenner, Martin. "The Appeal of Confiscation in Economic Development." *Economic Development and Cultural Change.* **3 (1954-55): 201-18; and, "Second Thoughts on Confiscation."** *Economic Development and Cultural Change.* **11 (July 1963): 367-71.**

Bronfenbrenner develops and estimates results for alternative models of economic development - with and without the confiscation of foreign assets. Working in the early 1950s, his model is based on the experience of the great social transformations, particularly the Russian Revolution of 1917. The model tests whether confiscation (nationalization of investment without payment of compensation brings the economic benefits often claimed.

From the political risk analyst's point of view, Bronfenbrenner lists eight factors that make the developing world less safe for foreign investment. These are (1) lower social mobility compared to Western Europe during its industrialization; (2) xenophobia; (3) a self-conscious haste about the industrialization process; (4) a tension between consumption and the Calvinist ethic of self-denial that facilitated capital accumulation in the West; (5) greater skill of Third World governments; (6) greater propensity for state ownership modeled on the socialist economies; (7) the lower legitimacy of private property; and, (8) greater organizational strength of labor that increases the difficulty of suppressing real wages during the drive to accumulate capital. If Western-based analysts had been alert to these differences, the expropriations of the 1960s and 1970s would have been less of a surprise.

Chandler, Geoffrey. "The Innocence of Oil Companies." *Foreign Policy.* **27 (Summer 1977): 52-70.**

A Director of the Shell Petroleum Company, Chandler brings a wealth of experience to bear in this and other pieces on the international oil industry. While his perspective is that of a participant, he correctly cautions against attributing too much power to the oil companies. He argues that the oil companies respond to events in their political, economic and social environments and are innocent of their causes. The perception of power held by mass and elite groups throughout the world is exaggerated and based on erroneous conclusions about distant events that evidences oil company power. The overthrow of Dr. Mossadegh is one such misperception according to Chandler. The success of the Iranian boycott was due less to the power of the "Seven

Sisters" than it was to the support offered by the United States and Great Britain, the availability of alternative sources of petroleum and an extreme lack of solidarity among the major oil producing countries of the Middle East.

During the formative years of OPEC, the majors were beset by overcapacity and the entrants of the independents into the market. These factors accounted, in part, for the decline in the real price of oil. This in turn prompted greater activism on the part of OPEC, further constraining the oil companies. Chandler does admit, that the behavior of the oil companies themselves did contribute to nationalism on the part of the host countries. The lack of good political and social sense and the formation of economic and social enclaves within the host countries worked against the desirable image of a good corporate citizen.

Chase-Dunn, Christopher. "The Effects of International Economic Dependence on Development and Equality: A Cross-National Study." *American Sociological Review.* **40 (December 1975): 720-38.**

Chase-Dunn presents an empirical analysis of the effects of international dependence on the economic and social performance of developing countries. Dependence is measured in terms of investment penetration and reliance on foreign capital for debt financing. Economic performance is measured by economic growth and internal inequality. Dependent variables are GNP per capita, electricity consumption, and percent of labor force in non-agricultural occupations. Control variables are domestic capital formation and extent of mining. Data from 1950 and 1970 are analyzed with panel regression techniques. Data for approximately thirty LDCs are drawn from the World Bank, the IMF, the *World Handbook of Political and Social*

Indicators, and other secondary sources. Both types of dependence have a negative effect on growth and a positive, though non-significant, effect on domestic inequality.

Cobbe, James H. *Governments and Mining Companies in Developing Countries.* **Boulder: Westview Press, 1979, p. 332.**

Cobbe focuses on the political and social factors that affect government-business relations in developing countries in the natural resource sector. The objectives of the international resources firm will almost certainly clash with those of the host government. The firm is following goals keyed to the profitability of a global enterprise. The host government pursues several objectives that are inconsistent with those of the multinational. These goals are political survival, maximizing a social/economic welfare function, and obtaining personal or ideological goals. Bargaining between the government and the firm occurs in the context of a resource that is ultimately (even with enhanced recovery technologies) exhaustible.

In the face of increased demands for local control, Cobbe admits the continuing need for foreign enterprise in this area. The vertical integration of the copper bauxite and iron industries require a continuing relationship between the producers of raw ores (be they corporate subsidiaries or state- owned enterprises) and downstream consumers of those ores. The uncertainty and high cost of exploration and development are other factors that require the continuing activity of the multinational enterprise.

Cobbe's method is the case study. Looking at Zambia (copper) and Botswana (nickel, copper, iron and diamonds) he argues against a general theory of Third World nationalism. "No general theory, capable of producing sharp hypotheses testable by reference to hard statistical data will emerge. The relationships involved seem too complex, the particularities of individual situations too important, and the methodology adopted to inexact, for that to be possible." (pp. 13–14).

The case studies are thorough, but are poorly integrated with the theoretical observations at the beginning of the book and do not, by the author's own statement, contribute much to a general theory of nationalism. Cobbes' conclusions parallel those of Moran and others about the bargaining strengths of multinationals and host countries. First, firm- government relations are complex but they can be understood with extant tools and methods. (pp. 277ff.) The key variables are the structure of the industry, the distribution of skills and information, and the objectives of firms and governments. Second, the explanation is not by economics alone. The role of domestic pressure groups, the desire of the government to maintain its power, and the independent effect of political or ideological objectives must be taken into account.

Cohan, A. S. *Theories of Revolution: An Introduction.* New York: John Wiley and Sons, 1975, p. 228.

Cohan reviews four basic approaches to the study of revolution. The Marxist approach argues that revolution results from changes in the structure of society. Revolutions are normal and inevitable. The functionalist approach (Talcott Parsons, Chalmers Johnson) focuses on the factors that enable societies to persist over time. Conflict is endemic but not inherent; it is undesirable and avoidable. The *mass society* approach (Hannah Arendt, William Kornhauser) argues that traditional social structures provide buttresses to the system. Modernization weakens these pillars of traditional society by questioning values and roles and bringing large groups into the political process for the first time.

The *psychological approach* is prominent in academic circles today and has deep historical roots. This approach focuses on the mental condition of individuals, particularly their dissatisfaction with existing conditions and their expectations about their likely future attainments. In the work of deTocqueville, Ted Robert Gurr, James C. Davies and others, the individual's perception of his *relative deprivation* is the driving engine of revolution. These authors build on individual discontent and examine the factors that lead to the politicization of that discontent and its actualization in political violence or revolutionary activity. The effect of relative deprivation on political stability is mediated by beliefs about the legitimacy and efficacy of political action/ political violence, the coherence and strength of groups that would provide a context for political action, the balance of coercive capacity of the government and opposition and the influence of forces external to the national political system.

Coronel, Gustavo. ***The Nationalization of the Venezuelan Oil Industry.*** **Lexington, Mass: Lexington Books, 1983, p. 292.**

This case study of the Venezuelan oil industry covers the period 1878 - 1983 and is based, largely, on published sources and interviews with government officials Any history of natural resources in Latin America begins with the premise that subsoil rights are vested in the state. State ownership of all subsoil resources dates back to the 1526 declaration of Charles I of Spain. The state has the authority to grant concessions for the development of these resources regardless of the ownership of surface. Coronel chronicles the development of the industry, paying close attention to the acceleration of change during the 1970–73 period, the influence of Libya and OPEC, the Venezuelan internal political debate over petroleum during 1974–75 and the nationalization of all foreign petroleum concessions in 1976.

Venezuela took the lead among the oil producing nations in adopting a policy of conservation. When full nationalization took place, the production of the Maracaibo fields had been in decline for several years. State ownership increased investment levels and the development of new fields. Expanded state oil revenues were fed into ambitious government development plans for the economy as a whole. Coronel traces the growth of national hydrocarbon firms to several common factors. First, host governments became more knowledgeable about the technical, commercial and financial aspects of the international petroleum industry. Second, through access to inexpensive domestic oil they were able to reduce their dependence on foreign firms, particularly the majors. Third, the hydrocarbon industry was a potent tool in the hands of governments for mobilizing political support and acquiring the economic resources to support ambitious development objectives.

Curry, Robert L. "Global Market Forces and the Nationalisation of Foreign-Based Export Companies." *Journal of Modern African Studies.* **14 (March 1976): 137-43.**

Curry focuses on the policies of mineral exporters in Black Africa during the 1970s. Key national policy goals include boosting employment, strengthening foreign exchange holdings, and increasing public revenues. Exporters that nationalize foreign investment in resource production are subject to global market forces that are beyond their individual control. This vulnerability explains the drive for cartelization. CIPEC *(Conseil intergovernemental des pays exportateurs de cuivre)* was formed by Zambia, Zaire, Peru and Chile in an attempt to maximize their control over the international copper industry. Control over the world supply and price of copper was essential if they were to realize gains from extensive nationalizations of foreign copper firms. However, CIPEC never accounted for enough of world copper production (without even taking substitutes into account) to attain its objectives. The recessions of the 1970s, the winding down of the U.S. space program, the slackening of the housing boom and the end of the Vietnam War coincided to reduce world demand for copper, crippling CIPEC.

Curry, Robert L., and Daniel Rothchild. "On Economic Bargaining Between African Governments and Multinational Companies." *Journal of Modern African Studies.* **12 (June 1974): 173-89.**

The bargaining power model of host country/investor relations is based on skills, flexibility, power, and experience. Curry and Rothchild argue that this model is affected by political impatience in the host country and reciprocal demand intensity (the range of alternatives available for the host country and the investor). Regional or global harmonisation of bargaining positions is recommended as one means of increasing LDC strength.

Das, Rajan. "Impact of Host Government Regulations on MNC Operations: Learning from Third World Countries." *Columbia Journal of World Business.* **16(1) (Spring 1981): 85-90.**

Das argues that the management of the multinational enterprise is complex, particularly in the areas of strategic planning, resource allocation and technology transfer. The issue of ownership of foreign subsidiaries, e.g. joint ventures with the host government or local private companies, is also an area of controversy.

India has taken a number of important measures to assert local control over multinational enterprises. The most significant of these are the Industries Development and Regulation Act of 1951, the Monopolies and Restrictive Trade Practices Act of 1969 and the Foreign Exchange Regulation Act of 1973. The intent of these acts is to increase Indian participation in the local operations of foreign-based companies and increase the flow of technology into the local economy.

Davies, James C. (ed). *When Men Revolt and Why*. New York: The Free Press, 1971, p. 357.

This edited collection contains 32 articles on the sources and effects of political instability and revolution. It has become a standard reference work on theory and methods in the area of instability research. Pieces by Aristotle, deTocqueville, Marx and Engels outline general theories of political change. The psychological antecedents of revolution are discussed by John Dollard and James Davies. Social science approaches, including cross- national quantitative analyses of the causes of revolution, are presented by Bruce M. Russett, Mancur Olson, Ivo and Rosalind Feierabend and Ted Robert Gurr. This articles deal respectively with the impact of land inequality on instability, socioeconomic change on stability, psychological frustration on aggressive political behavior, and causal modeling approaches to the analysis of civil strife.

Deutsch, Karl W. *Nationalism and Its Alternatives*. New York: Alfred A Knopf, 1969, p. 208.

Deutsch presents a theory of national integration and modernization based on the development of communication patterns within a country. These communication patters require a common language and shared historical experiences. These factors leading to national integration are missing in many Third World states. The type of sectarian or ethnic conflict witnessed in Lebanon or Nigeria, for instance, is not unexpected given the sharp and reinforcing cleavages evident in these nations. The experience of nation building in Western Europe, Eastern Europe and the Third World are contrasted. National integration in Western Europe began early, was slow paced and integrative. National development in Eastern Europe was late, fast paced and secessionist (i.e. due to the disintegration of the Russian, Austrian and Ottoman Empires). National development in the Third World is occurring later in a more crowded and self-conscious world, is fastest paced of all, and has been accompanied by bitter and violent struggles for independence and national political power once independence has been achieved.

Diaz, Ralph A. "The Andean Common Market: Challenge to Investors." *Columbia Journal of World Business.* **6(4), (July-August 1971): 22-28.**

The objective of the foreign investment legislation of the Andean Common Market (Bolivia, Chile, Colombia, Ecuador, Peru) was, over a period of fifteen years, to turn foreign-owned companies into mixed companies. Foreign investment in certain key sectors (banking, insurance) was prohibited altogether. Strict entry regulations and registration procedures were instituted to increase MNC responsiveness to regional development objectives. A Council of the Americas study showed that 51 of 56 member companies expected to be effected by ANCOM and that all 50 new investment projects planned for the region in 1970 were put on hold.

Doxey, Margaret. *Economic Sanctions and International Enforcement.* **London: Oxford University Press, 1971, p. 161.**

Doxey examines the history of economic warfare in the twentieth-century and concludes that economic sanctions are generally ineffective. Specific cases of warfare included embargoes and blockades during World Wars I and II, the Arab oil weapon, the Soviet and East European boycotts of Yugloslavia and Albania, the League of Nations embargo of Italy, and U.N sanctions against Portugal, South Africa, North Korea and Rhodesia. Sanctions often evoke stockpiling, the development of alternative sources and materials, evasion, reliance on "non-sanctionists" and the integration of public morale in the target state. Structural problems in sanctions include goal setting, selection of measures, determining the scope of sanctions, costs to the sanctioners, and the policing and supervising of sanctions.

Einhorn, Jessica Pernitz. *Expropriation Politics.* Lexington, Mass: D.C. Heath and Company, 1974, p. 148.

Einhorn assessed the U.S. reaction to the expropriation in Peru of the International Petroleum Company in 1968. A model of policymaking is developed based on Morton Halperin's *Bureaucratic Politics and Foreign Policy.* This model focuses attention on the bureaucratic players, their personal and institutional interests and values, and the extent to which executive agencies are able to act independently of the President. Bureaucratic politics will have more scope in economic issues compared to major national security issues because their salience is lower and the attention of the President will be less focused on international investment issues.

Elaid, H.H., and M.S. El-Hennawi. "Foreign Investment in LDCs: Egypt." *California Management Review.* 24(4), (Summer 1982): 85-91.

Third World governments need to provide incentives for multinational companies to invest. A survey of corporate executives elicited the factors important for a good investment climate in Egypt. Politial stability ranked high on the list as did government guarantees regarding expropriation and concessionary tax treatment. Barriers to investment in Egypt are high rates of inflation, inadequate communications and constantly changing regulations. Egypt's reputation for red tape remains strong among potential investors. The government must energetically dispel those concerns if it is to boost the quantity of foreign investment, particularly from the United States.

Faber, M., and J.G. Potter. *Towards Economic Independence: Papers on the Nationalisation of the Copper Industry in Zambia.* **New York and London: Cambridge University Press, 1971, p. 134.**

Faber and Potter examine corporate policies toward the copper belt, the recovery of their mining rights after nationalization, the future of Zambia's mining industry, an overview of the 51 percent equity takeover, and the evolution of the bargaining strengths of the state and the copper companies.

Fatemi, Nasrollah S., and Gail W. Williams. *Multinational Corporations: The Problems and the Prospects.* **London: Thomas Yoseloff, 1975, p. 290.**

The theme of this book is the assessment of the costs and benefits of multinational corporations for host countries and the policy implications of those assessments. The authors review the historical development of multinationals in terms of their impact on labor and employment, technology transfer, taxation, and the balance of payments.

Conflict between governments and companies arises over ownership, local sourcing of inputs, sovereignty over basic resources, and, in the U.S. case, antitrust policy and limitations on trading strategic goods. This last policy is specified in the 1917 Trading with the Enemy Act and the 1949 Export Control Act. The size, wealth and mobility of multinational corporations make them unusually powerful citizens in most host countries.

The Appendix contains UN resolutions on multinational corporations and extensive data tables.

Fayerweather, John (ed.). *Host National Attitudes Towards Multinational Corporations.* **New York: Praeger Publishers, 1982.**

This edited collection focuses on public opinion in several host countries toward multinational corporations. Elite opinion surveys and a content analysis of the press were undertaken in 1970–71 to measure attitudes in Great Britain, France, Canada, Mexico, Chile, Venezuela, Brazil and Nigeria. The authors conclude that elite beliefs about multinationals are a function of how such firms function within their society, national political culture, and the socioeconomic status of the respondent.

Flanagan, Robert J., and Arnold R. Weber (eds.). *Bargaining Without Boundaries: The Multinational Corporation and International Labor Relations.* **Chicago: University of Chicago Press, 1974, p. 258.**

Differing laws, policies and management styles pose problems for management and local labor when U.S. companies invest overseas. Union strategies range from bargaining within one country to coordinated international collective bargaining to protective legislation at the national level. Incentives for the unions to adopt an international approach are reviewed. Examples from the U.S. and Canada on the disruptive effects of foreign firms on local labor practices are detailed. Management approaches to local labor are discussed. Ford receives high marks for the priority it gives to national practices in the 30 countries where it manufactures automobiles.

Ford, Alan W. *The Anglo-Iranian Oil Dispute of 1951-52.* **Berkeley: University of California Press, 1954, p. 348.**

Ford describes the history of the Anglo-Iranian oil dispute. It provides an excellent case for the study of the role of law in international relations. Nineteenth-century confidence in the rule of law has been replaced by "political realism" and the undermining of expectations about lawful behavior in world politics. The interaction of politics and international law is presented up to the rejection of Great Britain's claims before the International Court of Justice in The Hague.

Frank, Isaiah. *Foreign Enterprise in Developing Countries.* **Baltimore: Johns Hopkins University Press, 1980, p. 199.**

Multinational managers recognize the diversity of the Third World and the need for flexibility in approaching each country on its own terms. Written questionnaires to 402 firms and in-depth interviews with managers from 90 multinationals yield information on perceptions of risk and sources of conflict between national governments and companies.

Companies were selected in-depth interviews based on their size, industry, geographic distribution of subsidiaries, ownership structure and size and level of development of the host country. Managers were interviewed from Japanese (17), U.S. (27), British (13), West German (9), Swedish (7), Australian (7), French (6), and Belgian, Italian, Swiss and Dutch (1) firms.

Sources of strain were instability, the growth in bargaining of the host governments, changing national goals (ideology?) and scapegoating. National goals were viewed by managers as inconsistent and poorly articulated. Industry was a stronger predictor of management views (e.g. petroleum vs. manufacturing) than was nationality.

Garnick, Daniel H. "The Appeal of Confiscation Reconsidered: A Gaming Approach to Foreign Economic Policy." *Economic Development and Cultural Change.* **11 (July 1963): 353-66.**

Garnick critically reviews Bronfenbrenner's work on the economic appeal of confiscation for developing countries. Garnick argues that Bronfenbrenner's approach is simplistic and misleading. The implicit two-player game (host country and foreign investor) in a zero sum situation with payoffs measured only in terms of foreign aid overlooks other relevant actors and forms of benefit. Other players are domestic economic actors, foreign countries and international organizations. Payoffs include, in addition to bilateral aid, multilateral aid, investment and trade concessions. Garnick varies Bronfenbrenner's assumptions and uses the revised model to generate different outcomes.

Ghadar, Fariborz. "Political Risk and the Erosion of Control: The Case of the Oil Industry." *Columbia Journal of World Business.* **17(3) (Fall 1982): 47-51.**

Ghadar follows Robock's earlier work and defines political risk as discontinuities in the national environment that are difficult to anticipate and that result from political change. Ghadar's theme is that much political risk arises from the loss of control over national economic life. Nationalization of the foreign investor is the last logical step in the long process of reasserting that authority.

Following the obsolescing bargain model, Ghadar argues that over time conflict between the host country and the foreign investor will focus on the amount of payments (royalties, taxes) for petroleum extracted, information collection about the industry so that the host government can set its own performance in perspective, and the development of an economic development agenda by the host. This development agenda may require that the host government make the basic decisions on output, price and marketing either through regulation or direct state ownership.

Control in the international petroleum industry is based on barriers to entry due to economies of scale, barriers to entry due to marketing and the availability of technology. The erosion of control differs in each major phase of the industry: crude extraction, refining, and marketing.

Girvan, Norman. "Making the Rules of the Game: Country-Company Agreements in the Bauxite Industry." ***Social and Economic Studies.*** **20 (December 1971): 378-419; and,** ***Corporate Imperialism, Conflict and Expropriation: Multinational Corporations and Economic Nationalism in the Third World.*** **White Plains, New York: M. E. Sharpe, 1976.**

The bauxite producing countries of the Caribbean and Latin America are the focus of Girvan's analysis of the relations between foreign investors and host governments. This paper is concerned with the development of specific operating agreements beginning in the 1960s. The approach is narrative and descriptive. The author concludes that the multinational-host country "relationship leads to a cumulative process of development and enrichment for aluminum companies, and the metropolitan countries where they are based, and a cumulative process of underdevelopment and dependence for the bauxite countries which provide most of the raw materials."

Host country regulations affect resource accessibility, operating conditions for foreign business, payments streams and the legal status of agreements themselves. Girvan concludes, however, that the power that the aluminum companies derive from their vertical integration is greater than the power that governments derive from their regulatory authority. The typical agreement for Girvan is "inherently subversive of national sovereignty."

Gobalet, Jeanne G., and Larry J. Diamond. "Effects of Investment Dependence on Economic Growth. ***International Studies Quarterly.*** **23(3) (September 1979): 412-444.**

The political risk facing multinationals is determined, in part, by perceptions in the host country of their contribution to the local economy. Gobalet and Diamond use cross-national data and advanced statistical tests to evaluate the effects of foreign investment on economic growth in developing countries. They conclude that, over the long-term, foreign investment dependence (defined in terms of earnings by foreign-owned subsidiaries over five-year periods beginning in 1950) has a strong negative effect on economic growth. This relationship is mediated by national wealth and power. More prosperous host countries have their economic growth less depressed by foreign investment dependence than do the poorest countries. Given Gobalet's and Diamond's measure of dependence, a key factor in host country perception of the foreigner's contribution will be the repatriation vs. the reinvestment of earnings.

Goodsell, Charles T. ***American Corporations and Peruvian Politics.*** **Cambridge: Harvard University Press, 1974, p. 272.**

Goodsell focuses on the political implications for Peru of the operations of large U.S. companies in that country over a long period of time. He reviews foreign investment and the activities of U.S. businesses in Peru specifically. The American business challenge to national sovereignty is discussed in terms of the extent of American control, the economic dependence of Peru and the political attitudes of U.S. business executives operating in the country. In 1974 there were approximately 300 U.S. firms in Peru and these were numbered among the largest in the country.

Corporate political behavior is examined in terms of its direct effects: access to policymakers, illegal payments, and public relations. The behavior of the U.S. Government is reviewed in terms of historical interventions, diplomatic conduct and economic sanctions. Bargaining processes between the government of Peru and foreign companies are analyzed for telecommunications, mining and petroleum.

Goodsell concludes that the most prevalent form of political activism is direct lobbying. Minor favors and contributions to political coffers are much less important than often believed. The goals of the multinational firms often overlapped with those of Peruvian entrepreneurs, landowners, industrialists and bankers. The Velasco revolution injured the interests of many Peruvians as well as those of international businesses. Finally, Goodsell concluded that company management dominated local political life in towns where the firm was the major employer.

Grant, C. H. "Political Sequel to the ALCAN Nationalization in Guyana: The International Aspects." ***Social and Economic Studies.*** **22 (June 1973): 249-71.**

The government of Guyana nationalized the Demarara Bauxite Company (DEMBA) on February 23, 1971. This nationalization was the result of an internal political crisis and the breakdown of negotiations with DEMBA rather than a planned program, in Grant's view. DEMBA's parent company, ALCAN, preferred a unilateral settlement to a negotiated compromise and persisted in this position despite its knowledge of the domestic political and social effects of this stance.

Grant, Ronald M. and E. Spencer Wellhofer (eds.). *Ethno-Nationalism, Multinational Corporations and the Modern State.* **Denver: University of Denver Monograph Series on World Affairs, 1979, p. 90.**

Grant and Wellhofer emphasize the role of multinational corporations in the making and unmaking of ethnic groups. Foreign investors open up new ethnic areas through their plant location and recruitment strategies. Investors can increase or dilute inequality based on ethnic divisions through their allocation of resources and effects on the international economic role of the host state.

Specific articles examine the effects of foreign investment and exposure to the world economy on ethnicity in Latin America, the Caribbean and Western Europe. In the last region, the decline of smokestack industries and persisting regional imbalances are generating demands among Scots, Welsh, Basques, Bretons and Walloons. All these ethnic groups are distinguished by cultural and linguistic factors, but share economic attributes as well.

Grayson, L. E. ***National Oil Companies*** **New York: John Wiley, 1981, p. 269.**

Grayson discusses the origins of state-owned oil companies, the relations between state and privately-owned companies, and the management techniques of the nationally-owned firms. Illustrations include CFP and Elf-Acquitaine in France, ENI in Italy, Veba in West Germany, Norway's STATOIL and Britain's National Oil Company. European Community energy and oil policies are reviewed.

Groves, Roderick T. "Expropriation in Latin America: Some Observations." ***Inter-American Economic Affairs.*** **23 (Winter 1969): 47-66.**

Groves comments on the avalanche of expropriations in Latin America following the Cuban revolution. Although the Cuban example may have inspired other countries, Groves puts the weight on indigenous factors: nationalism, pressures for development; and the selectivity of most expropriations. Groves assesses the implications for U.S. foreign policy, economic and policies and international legal norms. Common remedies (Hickenlooper, risk insurance) are discussed.

Gurr, Ted Robert. ***Why Men Rebel.*** **Princeton, N.J: Princeton University Press, 1970, p. 421.**

The relative deprivation theory of political conflict is advanced to explain the scope and intensity of collective protest and organized rebellion. Relative deprivation is defined as the individual's perception of a discrepancy between his value capabilities (what he is likely to get) and his value expectations (what he would like to get). Three forms of relative deprivation are postulated: decremental, progressive and aspirational. Progressive relative deprivation is similar to Davies' notion of the "J-Curve". Relative deprivation focuses on expectations of future attainments and desires at the individual level. Other elements in the theory concern the process by which such discontent finds expression in the collective political life of the society and is actualized into violent, as opposed to peaceful and constitutional activity.

While relative deprivation is the driving engine of Gurr's model of political instability, its impact is mediated by several factors. These include, but are not limited to, perceptions of the legitimacy and efficacy of political violence for obtaining goals, the coherence and organizational capacity of dissident organizations, the coercive capacity of the state and its willingness to repress dissent, and the availability of external support for the government and opposition.

Hawkins, Robert G., Norman Mintz, and Michael Provissiero. "Governmental Takeovers of U.S. Foreign Affiliates." ***Journal of International Business Studies.*** **7 (Spring 1976): 3-16.**

With the exception of Eastern Europe and Cuba, this is a worldwide analysis of the takeover of 170 U.S. foreign affiliates since World War II. Although no data are available in this or any other study on the value of nationalized firms, tables are presented on the distribution of takeovers by industry, degree of discrimination between U.S. and other foreign firms, the form of takeover (nationalization, expropriation, contract cancellation, forced sale), and the political circumstances at the time of the takeover (new regime, regime ideology).

The political factors receive due weight in this analysis. "A nationalistic regime uses expropriation of foreign firms as a visible tool to solidify power and popularity, despite potential or actual economic costs." Political factors, e.g. political stability, is more important than ideology. Less than half of the takeovers were associated with a leftist change in regime.

In terms of economic variables, the extractive industries (natural resources and petroleum) accounted for the greatest share. The most common mode of taking was the nationalization of an industry composed only of foreign firms. The authors observe that the takeovers were highly concentrated in a small number of developing countries (Chile, Algeria, Tanzania). This finding parallels those of other studies that have looked at the cross-national distribution of nationalizations of firms from all capital-exporting states (Kobrin, 1980; Jodice, 1980).

Hibbs, Douglas A. ***Mass Political Violence: A Cross- National Causal Analysis.*** **New York: John Wiley and Sons, 1973, p. 253.**

Hibbs examines the causes of political violence in this cross-national and quantitative study of 108 countries over the period 1948-67. Two dimensions of political violence are reviewed: Collective Protest (riots, protest demonstrations, and political strikes) and Internal War (armed attacks, political assassinations and deaths from domestic group violence). The basic data were taken from the second edition of the

World Handbook of Political and Social Indicators (Taylor and Hudson, 1972).

The major factors found useful in explaining the crossnational variance in the level of Collective Protest and Internal War were economic development, socioeconomic change, government repression and number of military coups, and cultural differentiation among the population as a whole.

Hischier, Guido,and Peter Heintz. "Political Regimes of Developing Countries Within the International Stratification System and the World Economy: Some Correlates of Regime Types." *Paper Presented at the Annual Meeting of the International Studies Association.* **(Cincinnati, March 24-27, 1982), p. 53.**

A typology of regimes is developed based on their political potential, economic power and political power. This typology is applied to developing countries during the period 1960 to 1977. Sixty-six countries are included yielding a total of 182 political regimes. The authors are concerned with the effect of integration into the world economy on the domestic political structures and stability of developing countries. An analysis of variance was performed to differentiate regime types by GNP, export and import structures and gross domestic investment.

Huntington, Samuel P. *Political Order in Changing Societies.* **New Haven: Yale University Press, 1968, p. 488.**

This extensive study of modernization, social change and political stability focuses on the *degree* rather than the *form* of government.

The degree of government in the face of challenges to its authority is a function of the political institutionalization of the society. Political institutions are organizations, values and recurring patterns of behavior that are widely valued and supported throughout the population. They provide channels for the expression of dissent and the enforcement of authoritative decisions taken by the state. Political institutions may be distinguished by their degree of adaptability, autonomy, coherence and complexity.

Ingram, George M. ***Expropriation of U.S. Property in South America: Nationalization of Oil and Copper Companies in Peru, Bolivia, and Chile.*** **New York: Praeger Publishers, 1974, p. 392.**

Ingram investigates the causes and consequences of expropriation through three intensive cases studies. The Peruvian taking of IPC is evaluated in the context of Peruvian domestic politics, the role of APRA, the 1962 coup, and U.S. - Peruvian relations. Bolivian economic nationalism is chronicled from the expulsion of Standard Oil of New Jersey through the nationalization of the tin mines in 1952 to the expropriation of Gulf Oil in 1969. The foreign domination of the Chilean copper industry is analyzed from the nineteenth-century. Chileanization and ultimate nationalization is reviewed in the context of Chile's economic development and domestic political life.

General causes of expropriation in all three cases include statism, ideology, economic performance of the host country, host country relations with the home country (no deterrent in these cases), the size and sector of the investment, political pressures for local control, profits, and political interference by the multinational. In Peru, specific factors leading to the nationalization of IPC included its political role, its declining bargaining power, and the general political-economic crisis experienced by Peru during the mid-1960s. In Bolivia, specific causes included dissatisfaction over contract terms, the size and area of Gulf's operations, and domestic political events in 1969. Chile's nationalization was the culmination of a trend of indigenization occurring within a democratic and constitutional context and enjoyed support throughout all sectors of Chilean society. The profits enjoyed by Kennecott and Anaconda (due largely to the 1955 *Nuevo Trato*), and their balance of payments effects were stimulating factors on the road to nationalization.

Ingram assesses the consequences of expropriation. Topics include compensation, political stability, economic performance, availability of foreign capital, the role of international financial institutions, and the actions of the U.S. Government in the Hickenlooper context.

Jackman, Robert W. "Dependence on Foreign Investment and Economic Growth in the Third World." *World Politics.* **34(2), (January 1983): 175-96.**

Jackman assesses the relations between the Third World "periphery" and the industrial West. Specifically, he tests the hypothesis that foreign direct investment has a negative impact on economic growth in host developing countries since 1960. The article includes a review of the issues and the recent empirical literature.

Seventy-two countries from all regions of the Third World are included in the regression analysis (Saudi Arabia, Kuwait and Libya are excluded for obvious reasons). Growth rates from 1960 to 1978 were computed from World Bank data and regressed on the level (1960) and change in foreign and domestic investment, population size, change in the crude birth rate, and the intitial level of wealth. The level of foreign direct investment was found to have no independent effect on growth but changes (increases) in foreign investment had a positive effect on growth.

Jodice, David A. "The Politics of Expropriation: Sources of Change in Latin American Regimes for Foreign Direct Investment in Natural Resource Extraction, 1968–76." *Paper Presented at the Annual Meeting of the International Studies Association.* **Toronto, March 21–24, 1979). p. 44.**

The propensity of 21 Latin American states to nationalize foreign direct investment in petroleum production and mining and smelting during the period 1968–76 is analyzed with cross-nationally comparable quantitative indicators. Data on host country characteristics (size, level of development, government capacity); investment characteristics (investment dominance, sectoral concentration of foreign investment, profit repatriation); and the country's status in the international system (concentration of export structures, foreign aid dependence), were used in this analysis. Quantitative data are supplemented with information from the U.S. Information Agency on Latin American public opinion towards the multinational corporation and examples drawn from major instances of political risk (Peru, Chile, Jamaica).

Jodice, David A. "Sources of Change in Third World Regimes for Foreign Direct Investment, 1968–76." *International Organization.* **34(2), (Spring 1980): 177–206.**

The propensity to nationalize foreign direct investment in natural resource extraction (petroleum production and mining and smelting) across 50 developing countries is analyzed with aggregate statistical data. Propensity to nationalize is defined as the percent of 1967 stock of foreign direct investment taken over by the host government in the subsequent nine years. Corrections for within period investment flows and payment (if any) of compensation have not been made.

This percentage measure ranges from 0 to 100. It was regressed on quantitative measures of the host country (economic size, level of development, government capacity and economic strain - measured as the instability of export earnings); investment characteristics (foreign direct investment dominance of the local economy, sectoral and parent ownership concentration of investment and the contribution of the foreign investor to the local economy - measured by profit repatriation); and the international status of the host country (trade and aid dependence). A theory of the political sources of nationalism is devised and tested with event data (political protest, internal war, government change) taken from the *World Handbook of Political and Social Indicators.* The utility of alternative models of investment risk were evaluated with regression techniques. Hypotheses were developed to address individual country deviations from the overall norm.

Jodice, David A. "Understanding Expropriation: Reply to Libby and Cobbe." *International Organization.* **35(4), (Autumn 1981): 745-54.**

This is a reply to a critique by Libby and Cobbe (1981) of an earlier piece on sources of resource nationalism in developing countries (Jodice, 1980). This response focuses on the conceptual framework presented to explain expropriation, the validity and reliability of the data presented, and the appropriateness and conclusiveness of the analytic methodology employed.

Johnson, Harry G. "A Theoretical Model of Economic Nationalism in New and Developing States." *Political Studies Quarterly.* **80(2), (June 1965): 169-85.**

For a political scientist nationalism is an integrating force. It can bind communities together at the national level or fracture them by causing sub-national loyalties to coalesce. For the economist, nationalism is also a force for change. But overall, it is a force for policies that "do not make sense". Drawing on the work of Anthony Downs, Albert Breton and Gary S. Becker, Johnson presents an eclectic theory of the causes and effects of economic nationalism in developing countries. Nationalism directs the country's resources into so-called strategic sectors and away from basic infrastructure and agriculture. These symbols of national integration (airlines, mines, petrochemical plants) may bolster the power of the governing regime, but they result in a lower level of national material welfare than would otherwise be the case. Such investments are justified locally in terms of the "psychic income" that they produce for elites and masses in the host country. These general and intangible benefits are independent from the tangible benefits that accrue to specific individuals and groups as a result of nationalization.

Johnson, Leland L. "U.S. Business Interests in Cuba and the Rise of Castro." *World Politics.* **17(1), (October 1964): 440-59.**

This study covers all industries operating in Cuba during the late 1950s as they became exposed to risk following the overthrow of the Batista regime. The approach is qualitative and historical. The evidence is derived from public and journalistic sources.

Sources of risk included the dominance of investment in Cuba by U.S. firms, the high share of US investment in Latin America accounted for by Cuba, and the sectoral concentration of U.S. investment in sugar and utilities. Both sugar and power generation were highly visible activities that touched the lives of much of the population either as workers or consumers.

Under pressure from the U.S. government, Castro successfully transferred the hatred that his followers felt for Batista onto U.S. investors and Washington. American businesses contributed to Cuban animosity through the refusal of three companies to refine Soviet oil and the cutting of the U.S. sugar quota. Business behavior accelerated Castro's move away from the U.S. and toward the Soviet Union.

Johnson, William A., and Richard E. Messick. "Veritical Divestiture of U.S. Oil Firms: The Impact on the World Oil Market." *Law and Policy in International Business.* **8 (1976): 963-89.**

Johnson and Messick assess the impact of proposed diversture of U.S. oil companies on consuming countries, the international industry and U.S. foreign policy. The authors describe how the OPEC cartel acts to maintain oil prices and concludes that OPEC and the major oil companies do not have a "commonality" of interests. Divesture is rejected because it would undercut the ability of the oil companies to mitigate the effects of an OPEC embargo as in 1973-74.

Kahler, Miles. "Political Regime and Economic Actors: The Response of Firms to the End of Colonial Rule." *World Politics.* **33(3), (April 1981): 383-412.**

This historical analysis focuses on the relationship between the economic system and the political regime at the national level. The concern is the relationship between capitalism and liberal democracy. The method for examining that relationship is an analysis of the behavior of multinational firms in developing countries during decolonization. An element of this analysis is problem of political exposure of multinational firms. Kahler suggests that political exposure is a function of the extent to which firms carry out governmental functions (social welfare, law and order, international diplomacy), extent of reliance on the government as a customer or source of capital; the prominence of the investment in terms of its sector and size; and, the choice of a metropolitan or "colonial" base for the headquarters of the multinational.

Knudsen, Harald. ***Expropriation of Foreign Private Investments in Latin America.*** **Bergen, Norway: Universitetsforlaget, 1974, p. 356, and "Explaining the National Propensity to Expropriate: An Ecological Approach."** ***Journal of International Business Studies.*** **5 (Spring 1974): 51-72.**

In these two pieces Knudsen examines the expropriation experience of foreign companies in Latin America during the period 1968-71. Although a Marxist perspective is avowed in the preface to the book-length study, it has little or no effect on the selection of evidence, the statistical analysis of the data or the drawing of conclusions. The author examines the factors causing expropriation at two levels: country characteristics and firm specific characteristics.

Macro or country factors that affect political risk include system stability, information variables (e.g. newspaper circulation), urbanization, labor unionization and the abundance of natural resources. All of these factors are conceptualized as continua and are measured with interval level data. Micro factors affecting vulnerability to political risk include firm size, sector, and the perception on the part of host country nationals of the economic contribution that the foreign investor is making.

The data are analyzed with regression and discriminant analysis techniques that are well explained and used with care. The statistical results are very successful in terms of their ability to capture the effects of national and industry variables on propensity to expropriate. A major limitation of the study is the sparse data on corporate practices elicited through a mail questionnaire and the omission of numerous instances of expropriation from the primary database.

Kobrin, Stephen J. "The Environmental Determinants of Foreign Direct Manufacturing Investment: An Ex Post Empirical Analysis." *Journal of International Business Studies.* **(Fall-Winter 1976):**

The flow of direct investment in manufacturing is examined for sixty-two countries worldwide during the 1960s. Two measures are used: the number of new subsidiaries as reported by the Harvard Multinational Enterprise Project and the stock of manufacturing investment end 1967 as reported by the Organization for Economic Cooperation and Development. The approach is cross-national, comparative, quantitative and relies on such statistical tools as factor analysis and multiple regression.

The relationship between investment flows and the economic, social and political aspects of the host environment are examined. Kobrin concludes that the bulk of the explanation of cross-national variance in investment flows is due to economic factors. Political instability is not important per se. What is important are the ramifications for business of policy discontinuities arising out of the political process.

Kobrin, Stephen J. "When Does Political Instability Result in Increased Investment Risk?" *Columbia Journal of World Business.* **(Fall 1978): 113-122.**

Political instability consistently ranks high as a concern of top level managers of American-based multinational corporations. A review of corporate practices of analyzing instability in the investment decision process reveals that a rigorous and systematic assessment is the exception rather than the rule. Political assessments tend to be superficial and impressionistic. Given management reliance on the views and opinions of local or regional executives and the elite newspapers in the home countries, this is not surprising. Kobrin argues that this results in an overstatement of political risk and a loss of opportunities due to the excess caution such misperceptions can generate.

Kobrin goes on to analyze the effects of instability on investment risk. Using manufacturing investment as a test case, the direct and indirect effect of political instability on the investment climate are examined. Working with forty-eight developing countries during the 1960s, Kobrin examines the residual of investment (positive or negative) from what would be expected given "normal economic conditions". This residual value is a function of political turmoil, internal war and intra-elite struggles.

Kobrin, Stephen J. "Foreign Enterprise and Forced Divestment in the LDCs." *International Organization.* **34(1), (Winter 1980): 65-88.**

This article reports the first stage of a project on the firm and industry factors that affect vulnerability to economic nationalism. Covering the period 1960–76 (subsequently extended to 1979) a total of 1,535 subsidiaries were expropriated in 511 distinct acts in seventy-six developing countries. Abstracting from instances of social revolution (Kobrin's "mass takers") it is possible to assess vulnerability to risk at the level of the affiliate. Expropriation is a policy tool for asserting local control over foreign business in the pursuit of short- term and long-run political objectives on the part of host country elites. Given this rational basis it not surprising that systematic conclusions can be drawn about factors affecting risk. Kobrin's study indicates that sector and ownership structure are the the most important factors affecting vulnerability.

Kobrin, Stephen J. "The Nationalization of Oil Production, 1919-80." *Paper Presented at a Conference on Risk and Return in Large-Scale Natural Resource Projects.* **(Bellagio, Italy: November 1982), p. 48.**

This paper analyzes the policies of oil exporting nations toward foreign oil companies since 1919 and includes a unique comprehensive listing of oil nationalizations through 1980. Kobrin adopts the Hegelian notion of dialectical change to explain the long-term erosion of corporate control over the production, processing and marketing of petroleum products on an international basis. The erosion of the oil companies *strategic control* became undeniable after 1970 even though its recognition was delayed. Radical changes in the structure of the oil industry, the emergence of state-owned petroleum enterprises, the growth of independents, and the role of the Soviet Union as an oil exporter all contributed to this erosion of control. There was also a major shift in the nature of national objectives on the part of the oil producing countries from increasing their financial returns to asserting local control over operations.

Kobrin, Stephen J. "Diffusion as an Explanation of Oil Nationalization." (New York, July 1983, unpublished paper), p. 47.

This paper tests a diffusion hypothesis of oil nationalizations throughout the Third World during the period 1960–79. During this 20 year period there were 43 nationalizations in 24 countries. Poisson and Contagious Poisson distributions were fitted to the actual distribution of takings on an annual basis by country. The pattern of oil nationalizations is consistent with the diffusion hypothesis even though proximate causes vary from case to case. Nationalizations after 1970 differed in motive, success and effect from those conducted before 1970.

Kobrin, Stephen J. ***Foreign Direct Investment, Industrialization and Social Change.*** **Greenwich, Connecticut: JAI Press, 1977, p. 188; and, "Foreign Direct Investment, Industrialization and Social Change."** ***Journal of Conflict Resolution.*** **20 (September 1976): 497–522.**

Working at the intersection of political science, development economics, and international business, Kobrin examines the impact of foreign direct investment and industrialization on development and social modernization. A quantitative, cross-national study of 59 countries uses additive and interactive regression models to estimate the effects of industrialization and foreign direct investment on three dimensions of modernity: role differentiation, mobility and social organization.

Krasner, Stephen D. *Defending the National Interest: Raw Materials Investments and U.S. Foreign Policy.* **Princeton N.J: Princeton University Press, 1978, p. 404.**

Krasner develops and tests three perspectives on U.S. policy in the area of foreign investment protection during the twentieth-century: Marxist, liberal and mercantilist or state-centric. The Marxist, or structured-Marxist approach looks at U.S. policy as the direct tool of international capitalism. The liberal perspective argues that state policy is the result of interest group bargaining that includes private corporations but is not limited to such economic actors. Both the Marxist and liberal perspectives argue that the state has little automony from social forces in setting national objectives and setting policies. The state-centric approach allocates substantial autonomy to the institutions of the central government and specific policymaking elites. These elites have, in Krasner's view, followed a consistent and stably ordered set of policy objectives during much of the twentieth-century. These objectives in the area of international political economy are (1) opposition to the international expansion of communism; (2) stability of sources of supply of key commodities; and, (3) enhancing competition in raw materials markets (antitrust, opposition to commodity cartels).

Krasner concludes that general foreign policy goals (national security, anti-communism) have consistently prevailed over the narrower economic goals of security of supply and competitive markets. He attributes this to the relative isolation of policymaking elites form social forces in this issue area and the divergence of business interests. For example, companies doing business in Peru were not supportive of a strong U.S. reaction to the nationalization of IPC by the Velasco government in 1968. They were, in effect, hostages to an accomodating U.S. response to the Peruvian nationalization of IPC.

Krasner, Stephen J. "Transforming International Regimes: What the Third Wants and Why." *International Studies Quarterly.* **25(1), (March 1981): 119-48.**

Krasner hypothesizes that the international and domestic weakness of Third World states leads them to try to change international regimes. Their weakness is evidences in the low share of direct tax revenues as a proportion of GNP and the relatively high share of GNP accounted for by the international trade sector. Both these measures indicate that, overall, Third World states have relatively less control over their domestic economies that developed countries and they are more vulnerable to changes in the international economy.

Third World states have captured the structure of international organizations created by the United States after World War II (one country, one vote). Their goals are to change the nature of the game (the international regime) rather than to better their share under the existing set of rules and procedures. Dependence has had a unifying effect on Third World view, with the exceptions of the OPEC countries and those that have successfully nationalized foreign direct investments in critical sectors.

LaPalombara, Joseph, and Stephen Blank. *Multinational Corporations and National Elites: A Study in Tensions.* **New York: The Conference Board, 1976, p. 124.**

For Canada and Italy, LaPalombara and Blank examine the historical role and current setting of foreign investment. Multinationals are currently under siege because of local perceptions of dependence, problems of national identity, pressures for equity ownership and joint ventures with local companies, and localization of research and development. Operational problems facing the firm include labor and industrial relations, organization and management, government relations and political analysis, reconciliation to codes of conduct, and extraterritoriality. LaPalombara's and Blank's conclusions (pp. 79–82) on the corporate use of political analysis are pessimistic. Senior management is not convinced of the need for long- term, systematic and comparative political analysis. When more than superficial political analysis is conducted, it occurs at entrance into a new country or divestment. These are points of crisis or decision and bias political analysis away from systematic and regular scanning of foreign political processes.

LaPalombara, Joseph, and Stephen Blank. *Multinational Corporations and Developing Countries.* **New York: Conference Board, 1979, p. 215.**

LaPalombara and Blank review the debate over sources of development, the role of foreign direct investment in LDCs, responses of LDC governments to foreign firms, and patterns of LDC policies. Host government policies include entrance screening, actions directed at ownership, management and employment, increased taxation and regulation of financial transactions and inter-agency administration of investment legislation. Their analytic model of political risk assessment includes host country politics, government policy, and elite-mass perceptions of the benefit that the foreign investor brings in addition to economic and financial factors. This framework is applied to Brazil, Malaysia and Nigeria.

Litvak, Isaiah A., and Christopher J. Maule (eds.). *Foreign Investment: The Experience of Host Countries, p. 409.* **New York: Praeger, 1970.**

The issues are defined in terms of economic effects, political activities, stimulation of sociocultural changes, and the nature of the legal environment of foreign investment. Case studies include Australia, Belgium, Canada, France, Japan, Norway, South Africa, the U.K, and, in the developing world, Argentina, India, Tunisia, Spain and Yugloslavia. Raymond Mikesell presents an overview article on extractive investment in developing countries.

Litvak, Isaiah A., and Christopher J. Maule. "Forced Divestment in the Caribbean. *International Journal.* **32 (Summer 1977): 501-32.**

The nationalization of the Reynolds Guyana Mines, Ltd. by Guyana on January 1, 1975 is the focus of this study. The nationalization is compared to the earlier divestment of ALCAN's subsidiary (DEMBA) and was the inevitable result of irreconcilable bargaining positions. The authors examine the proposals of DEMBA and the Government in order to shed light on tensions between the government and the private investor in the areas of social responsiblity and managerial control.

Litvak, Isaiah A., and Christopher J. Maule. "Nationalisation in the Caribbean Bauxite Industry." *International Affairs.* **51 (January 1975): 43-59.**

This article focuses on the 1971 nationalization of the Demarara Bauxite Company (DEMBA) which was a subsidiary of ALCAN. The authors explain why the Canadian government did not act to protect ALCAN's interests. First, ALCAN's dependence on Guyana as a source of bauxite was decreasing. Second, the government did not want to worsen Canada's already poor image in the Caribbean. Third, Canada lacked economic leverage. Fourth, as a major commodities producer herself, Canada was sensitive to Third World concerns. Fifth, as ALCAN was 40 percent U.S.-owned, there was an internal Canadian political debate over the appropriateness of a Canadian response.

Litvak, Isaiah A., and Christopher J. Maule. "Foreign Corporate Social Responsibility in Less Developed Economies." *Journal of World Trade Law.* **9 (March-April 1975): 121-35.**

The authors contrast the experiences of ALCAN Aluminum, Ltd. and Booker McConnell - UK in Guyana during the 1960s and 1970s. ALCAN's extremely negative experience is traced, by Litvak and Maule, to the company's attentiveness to its shareholders while the more successful Booker McConnell was concerned with the wellbeing of its shareholders, employees, customers and the community as a whole.

Corporate social responsibility arises in developing countries from the expected contribution of FDI to local development objectives. Expectations will be higher in countries where growth is keyed to one or two industries and where those key industries are highly concentrated. The extent to which corporations will be able to satisfy these national expectations is keyed to the corporation's underlying business philosophy. Litvak and Maule recommend a strategy based on international integration of corporate activities, the indigenization of management at the local level, the avoidance of a labor aristocracy (ALCAN's wellpaid miners were all of African descent), and the treatment of government/community relations as a key management function.

Mahler, Vincent A. *Dependency Approaches to International Political Economy: A Cross-National Study.* **New York: Columbia University Press, 1980, p. 218.**

The theme of this study is that underdevelopment is the systematic result of asymmetrical relations between the developing countries and the industrial states. Seventy countries are included in this quantitative test of theories of international imperialism. Countries are drawn from Black Africa, the Middle East, Latin America, Asia and Southern Europe. Mahler examines the modes of dependence: foreign direct investment; trade ties; aid dependence; financial debt; and, military and educational ties. The effects of dependence are evaluated for the following areas of LDC performance: welfare; unemployment; economic growth and distribution. Controls for level of development and natural resource endowment were introduced into multiple regression models of the the dependency–wellbeing process.

Mikesell, Raymond F. *Foreign Investment in the Mineral and Petroleum Industries -- Case Studies of Investor–Host Country Relations.* **Baltimore: Johns Hopkins University Press, 1971, p. 459.**

This edited collection reviews the contribution of petroleum and mining to development, the taxation of extractive industries in developing countries, labor relations, the relationship of foreign petroleum companies and the state in Venezuela, the impact of the petroleum industry on Venezuelan exports, the effect of the oil industry on Argentina's self- sufficiency, the evolution of the Aramco concession, the oil industry and the Iranian economy, sulphur mining in Mexico, iron ore in Brazil and Venezuela, and the historical development of the Chilean copper industry since 1922.

Mikesell, Raymond F. *Foreign Investments in Mining Projects.* **Cambridge, Mass: Oelgeschlager, Gunn and Hain, 1983, p. 295.**

Mikesell analyzes the nature and evolution of modern mining agreements. He focuses on the issues related to the division of economic rents between the host country and the foreign firm. These issues include the taxation of corporate profits, calculation of taxable income, excess or windfall profits taxes, mandatory government equity participation, royalties and export taxes, import duties, tax stability, debt/equity ratios and the payment of interest on debt. Other issues include the government approval process, questions on environmental impact, marketing, and local sourcing, employment and training. Case studies include the copper, nickel, iron, and gold industries in Chile, Guatemala, Panama, Papua New Guinea, Botswana, Peru, Indonesia, Brazil and Colombia.

Mikesell, Raymond F. *Foreign Investment in Copper Mining: Case Studies of Mines in Peru and Papua New Guinea.* **Baltimore: Johns Hopkins University Press, 1975, p. 143.**

This study focuses on investment decision-making and contract negotiation in the international copper industry. Factors considered are profitability criteria, cash-flow analysis, rates of return, price projections, and the minimum expected rate of return. Political risks are briefly considered (pp. 18–21). Political risk can be assessed in terms of the host country's recent history, policies of the current government, and the probability of a revolutionary change in government. Mikesell suggests that diversification is the most effective means for offsetting risk. He admits, however, that geographical diversification is seldom an option in copper where reserves are concentrated and an open-pit, low-grade mine requires approximately $750 million (1975 dollars) to open.

Monsen, R. Joseph and Kenneth D. Walters. ***Nationalized Companies: A Threat to American Business.*** **New York: McGraw-Hill Book Company, 1983, p. 178.**

This study reviews the growth of state-owned enterprises in the U.K., France, Italy, West Germany, Norway, Sweden and Austria. Sectors include steel, railroads, energy (coal and oil), transportation, banking, airlines and posts and telecommunications. The research is based on interviews with corporate executives and government officials and international statistical comparisons of the scope of governmental activity. Monsen and Walters assess the possible impact of the growth of West European state companies on the United States. In the U.S., rail services have been nationalized in a *de facto* sense. The Lockheed and Chrysler bailouts have parallels in West European industry. Electoral pressures increase the appeal of nationalization as U.S. politicians try to save ailing industries.

Even though the state owns the corporations, the problem of control remains. The authors argue that the state controls the ends, the management of the enterprise controls the means. Management proposes, government disposes. If the government's political welfare is at stake, it will retain effective control. Techniques of control include appointments, direct intervention and financial controls. The lack of political skills is the single most important cause of failure on the part of managers of state-owned enterprises. This failure is two-edged. Managers have difficulty maintaining their autonomy from ministers but also lack the skills to obtain what they need from the political process.

Moran, Theodore H. ***Multinational Corporations and the Politics of Dependence: Copper in Chile.*** **Princeton, N.J: Princeton University Press, 1974, p. 286.**

This case history focuses on the development of copper policy in Chile from 1945 to the overthrow of the Allende government in September 1973. The author blends political and economic styles of analysis in order to portray the interaction of two systems: the international copper industry including its operations in Chile, and domestic interest groups giving voice to increasing demands for greater Chilean control over key resources and the reversal of a pattern of *dependencia* that many believed was constraining Chile's economic and political development.

The interaction of these two systems is characterized by the obsolescing bargain model of host country -- foreign investor relations. This model assumes that change is the only constant in this relationship and that the direction and pace of change in natural resource extraction can be understood and predicted by observing several key variables. These variables include the sophistication of the host government's bureaucracy, the division of national opinion on the desirability of foreign ownership of natural resources, market conditions (demand, supply, substitutability), the degree of competition in the copper industry, and the dependence of any particular copper firm on its local (Chilean) operations. This dependence of the multinational enterprise on resources from a given country enhances the bargaining power of the host government. Other actors that effect this interaction include the home government of the copper firm and downstream customers for the firm's product.

Moran, Theodore H. "The Alliance for Progress and 'The Foreign Copper Companies and Their Local Conservative Allies' in Chile: 1955-1970." *Inter-American Economic Affairs.* **25 (Spring 1972): 1-25.**

A natural alliance between foreign investors and local conservative forces was ruptured in Chile because of the conflicting priorities of the Alliance for Progress. The Alliance proposed sweeping land and tax reforms, economic development via private interests, and that all of the above would be accomplished with security or at least equitable treatment for American investors. The goals of the Alliance drove a wedge between Kennecott, Anaconda, and potential Chilean allies that eventually produced widespread demands for nationalization.

Morley, Samuel A. "What to Do About Foreign Direct Investment: A Host Country Perspective." *Studies in Comparative International Development.* **10 (Spring 1975): 45-69.**

Morley proposes a set of criteria for treating foreign direct investment (FDI) in order to maximize national welfare. Government intervention is justified because LDC markets are not competitive and profit maximization by multinationals imposes direct costs on host economies. Morley recommends (1) that foreign firms be prohibited from sectors where they have no cost advantage, (2) that FDI be accepted if its products are complicated and where expertise cannot be bought "off-the-shelf", and, (3) that multinationals not be granted permanent tax concessions.

Newman, William H. "Adapting Transnational Corporate Management to National Interests." *Columbia Journal of World Business.* **14(2), (Summer 1979): 82-88.**

Under the auspices of the International Academy of Management, questionnaires were sent to Fellows in thirty-nine countries. Sixty-four responses were received. Two-thirds of those managers responding expected greater levels of conflict between transnational corporations and governments. Sources of conflict included local ownership, profit sharing on non-renewable resources, local employment, technology transfer, foreign exchange effects of foreign investment, and political activities by transnationals in local politics. Proposals for changes in managerial strategy include the delegation of greater responsibility to local management and the indigenization of management at the affiliate level.

North, Christoper M. "Risk Minimization for International Lending in Regional Banks." *Columbia Journal of World Business.* **16(4), (Winter 1981): 21-27.**

There are four types of risk in international lending. These are credit, legal and documentation, funding and country risks. Credit risks are evaluated in the light of the prospective borrower's character, the capacity to repay, and collateral for the loan. Country risk is evaluated in terms of the exchange rate and possible exchange controls, sovereign risk (governmental refusal to honor its debts), and general risks arising from international or civil war.

Regional bank exposure to risk is reviewed. Banks can reduce their vulnerability to risk by operating on the following variables: international distribution of loans, country and nature of borrower, currency and security of credit, spreads and fees, and the quality of its own political risk analysis.

Olson, Richard Stuart. "Expropriation and Economic Coercion in World Politics: A Retrospective Look at Brazil in the 1960s." *Journal of the Developing Areas.* **13(3), (April 1979): 247-62.**

The expropriation of U.S.-owned utility companies in the Brazilian state of Rio Grande do Sul in 1959 and 1962 is the subject of this article on investment protection. Olson draws on Galtung's work on dependency and sanction effectiveness in this analysis of U.S. responses to these nationalizations. Negative, collective and public sanctions are more likely to cause national integration than a collapse of the target state. U.S. policy at that time aimed at subdividing the political elite of Brazil, targeting Goulart, while maintaining political and economic support for the Brazilian military.

Olson, Richard Stuart. "Economic Coercion in International Disputes: U.S. and Peru in IPC Expropriation Dispute of 1968-71." *Journal of the Developing Areas.* **9 (April 1975): 395-414.**

Olson resolves a number of questions about the IPC case. Why did Belaunde compromise with IPC after years of dispute? Why did the military overthrow Belaunde and expropriate IPC? What were the strategies used in the confrontation by Velasco, IPC and the U.S. government? What effect did the Peruvian strategy of isolating the IPC case have on the perceptions of U.S. policymakers? Olson concludes that a general condition of dependency in the developing areas can be modified by state action. Nationalization of foreign investment can reduce the dependence of a Third World country on the international economy. The effectiveness of such an expropriation will depend, in part, on the tactics adopted by the host government after nationalization.

Olson, Richard Stuart. "Expropriation and International Economic Coercion: Ceylon and the West 1961-65." *The Journal of the Developing Areas.* **11(2), (January 1977): 205-26.**

Ceylon (now Sri Lanka) nationalized American and British firms engaged in petroleum distribution during the early 1960s. Ceylon was the only Third World country nationalizing U.S. investments that was the target of the Hickenlooper Amendment. Working with public documents and data on foreign aid, loans and country economic performance, Olson demonstrates how the investment crisis exacerbated Ceylon's economic problems due to the commodity concentration of its exports and declining terms of trade. The author concludes that the effectiveness of sanctions is enhanced when they are applied against countries already undergoing economic distress.

Park, Tong-Whan, Farid Abolfathi and Michael Ward. "Resource Nationalism in the Foreign Policy Behavior of Oil-Exporting Countries, 1947-74" ***International Interactions.*** **2 (1976): 247-62.**

This paper analyzes the expropriation of petroleum production investments in Iran, Saudi Arabia, Kuwait, Algeria and Libya in the context of these countries' overall foreign policy behavior between 1947 and 1974. The analysis is based on data derived from two international events data projects: World Event Interaction Survey (WEIS) and Comparative Research on Events of Nations (CREON). From these large datasets a subset of events was pulled that related to petroleum policy. Sources of information included the *New York Times* and the *Middle East Journal.* Data are aggregated on a quarterly basis with codes for the intensity and content of target specific actions. "Resource nationalism is defined as the verbal and/or behavioral assertion of national interests and control in extractive industries." (p. 247)

The analysis proceeds from the inspection of quarterly line plots. The authors argue for the influence of special international events (formation of OPEC, Arab-Israeli Wars, government change in nationalist or radical directions) and the importance of international learning curves (diffusion). The paper argues for these conclusions on the basis of the time- series plots but does not statistically test hypotheses on the correlates of resource nationalism.

Peninou, Georges et al. *Multinational Corporations and European Public Opinion.* **New York: Praeger Publishers, 1978, p. 205.**

This analysis was sponsored by the European Centre for Study and Research on Multinational Corporations (ECSIM) and is based on two mass opinion surveys (1974, 1976) carried out in Denmark, the Netherlands, France, Great Britain, Belgium, Italy, West Germany, Luxembourg, and Ireland, under the auspices of the European Community, and a set of elite interviews obtained during April - May 1974 from Britain, France, West Germany, and the Netherlands.

Opinion surveys about multinational corporations dealt with several issues: public awareness of companies, nationality attributed to these major firms, perceptions of their attributes (e.g., efficient, gigantic, dangerous), advantages and disadvantages, the desirability of their activities expanding in Europe, etc.

This study provides an example of the utility of survey research to those who want to better understand foreign environments for international business. The blend of mass publics, general opinion leaders and shapers, and corporate executives is particularly appropriate. It dulls the frequent complaint that public opinion does not matter and provides a systematic look at those decisionmakers who directly affect the business climate.

Peterson, C.R. "Can Multinationals Survive in Today's World?" *Risk Management.* **28(2), (February 1981): 34–37.**

Peterson argues that political risk facing U.S. and foreign multinationals is increasing. While the pace of expropriation may have slowed, other forms of risk are on the rise. The tax implications of confiscation in developing countries are unclear. Risk can be offset through the use of private or public risk insurance. Insurance costs are country and project specific. Rates are highest for Third World countries.

Petras, James F. "Chile: Nationalization, Socioeconomic Change and Popular Participation." *Studies in Comparative International Development.* **8 (Spring 1973): 24–51.**

This study of the Chilean copper industry and its interaction with labor between the 1950s and 1973 is based on a series of structured interviews with four different groups: copper miners, copper technicians, copper management, and workers in agriculture. Petras examines the factors that enable the workers' movement to transform the business orientation of the movement into class consciousness. The circumstances of a nationalization will affect this process. Labor's class consciousness will be enhanced if there is mobilization and politicization prior to the divestment of the foreign company. Unlike the radical workers at El Teniente who saw nationalization as an opportunity for the redistribution of the benefits of the copper industry, workers at Chuquicamata did not become radicalized. Petras attributes their business unionism to their geographic isolation and relatively higher salaries.

Petras, James F., Morris Morley, and Steven Smith. ***The Nationalization of Venezuelan Oil.*** **New York: Praeger, 1977, p. 173.**

This study examines capitalist development in an historical perspective. Nationalizations in the Third World are reviewed in terms of their impact on development and U.S. policy. Chronologies of governments in Venezuela since 1870 and of Venezuelan oil initiatives are presented. The authors argue, in a Marxist vein, that economic and social development cause assertion of local control in the form of expropriation. They describe and analyze plans and programs for national capitalist development.

Pinelo, Adalberto J. ***The Multinational Corporation as a Force in Latin American Politics: A Case Study of the International Petroleum Company in Peru.*** **New York: Praeger, 1973, p. 171.**

Pinelo reviews the origins of the oil fields at *La Brea y Parinas*, the role of the International Petroleum Company in Peruvian politics, the nature of the players in local politics (parties, the military, the social oligarchy), the agreement between IPC and Belaunde, and the end of Belaunde, IPC and democratic reform with the Velasco coup.

Poynter, T. A. "Government Intervention in Less Developed Countries: The Experience of Multinational Companies." ***Journal of International Business Studies.*** **13(1), (Spring/Summer 1982): 9-25.**

Poynter focuses on government intervention rather than political risks. Risks are assessed in terms of how government policies affect corporate behavior, rather than events in the general political environment. Forms of intervention that were most common were international exchange restrictions, production levels and prices, and labor practices. Less frequent risk events include harassment from host country bureaucrats, ownership, and controls on intra- company product flows.

Managers of 104 subsidiaries in Tanzania, Kenya, Zambia, and Indonesia responded to written questionnaires on government risk events between 1970 and 1975. Poynter explains government intervention in terms of relative bargaining power (skills, flexibility, economic leverage) of governments and companies. Interventions are selective; host governments focus on specific firms. They are characterized as varying levels of enforcement of existing policies. Interventions are a function of the operating and managerial complexity of the subsidiary, the company's market orientation, the extent of local sourcing, the porportion of foreigners in managerial and technical positions, the strategic importance of the subsidiary's economic activity, and significantly, the politicial behavior of the subsidiary.

Purcell, Susan Kaufman. "Business- Government Relations in Mexico: The Case of the Sugar Industry." *Comparative Politics.* **13(2), (January 1981): 211-34.**

The author bases the analysis of political risk on the observation that in times of crisis the Mexican political elite maintains stability be giving priority to political over economic objectives. In times of crisis, elites promote the expansion of state control over the economy. The sugar industry is a major foreign exchange earner, accounts for approximately 12 percent of employment and GNP, and has been subjected to steady encroachment by the state. The political implications of a failure in that industry are severe. Approximately 300,000 family heads are employed in the industry. Government-business relations in this area are a classic case of the state taking over a declining industry to protect its political base, rather than taking over an economic winner that would strengthen the financial power of the government.

Ray, Dennis M. "Causes of Expropriation of American Companies Abroad." *Stanford Journal of International Studies.* **11 (Spring 1976): 122-52.**

Ray reviews the expropriation experience of American companies throughout the developing world since World War II. He describes a set of ninety-eight takings, most of which were in natural resource extraction. Compared with other data oriented approaches (Kobrin, 1980), this dataset underestimates the extent of nationalization in the Third World. Factors causing expropriation are nationalism which targets the *foreign* investor; political instability which impels governments to undertake symbolic actions against the multinational; the obsolescence of bargains originally struck under very different circumstances; perceptions of exploitation on the part of host country elites; and, development objectives that require the assertion of local control over key economic players.

Ray, James Lee, and Thomas Webster. "Dependency and Economic Growth in Latin America." *International Studies Quarterly.* **22 (September 1978): 409-34.**

This article empirically assesses the impact of wealthy capitalist states on eighten developing countries. Aggregatee economic indicators are developed and used for the 1960-70 period. Changes in per capita GNP are a function of the partner concentration of exports, the level of U.S. foreign direct investment, foreign and local investment as a percent of GNP, and external factor payments on foreign investment. The use of panel regression techniques reveals a positive relationship between dependence and economic growth in Latin America during the 1960s.

Riner, Deborah L. Private Banks and the Politics of Economic Policy-Making in Peru and Chile. *Paper Presented at the Annual Meeting of the American Political Science Association.* **(Denver, September 2-5, 1982): p. 23.**

These case studies analyzed the growth of private international borrowing in Peru and Chile that resulted, respectively, from U.S. reactions to nationalizations and human rights violations. International borrowing is also a function of domestic political factors. Foreign borrowing was the perfect solvent for political conflict: foreign funds were easily available and their costs mostly to be paid in the future. (p. 18) The growth of the Eurodollar and petrodollar markets during the 1970s enabled the large commercial banks to virtually replace the Bretton Woods organizations as the major source of funds. The expansion of private-sector borrowing affords developing countries more flexibility in the short-run. But over the long-term, indebtedness will increase the leverage of foreign lenders over the policies of borrowing states. The growth of debtor influence as a function of the size of their debt is not considered.

Robock, Stefan H. "Political Risk: Identification and Assessment." *Columbia Journal of World Business.* **6 (July 1971): 6-20.**

Robock indicates that political risk is a pervasive condition of conducting business overseas and that it is not limited to just developing countries. Writing in 1971, he argued that "...one of the challenges facing the international manager is to develop techniques for evaluating and forecasting political risk so that political risk elements can be included in decision-making on a more objective basis." (p. 6). The sources of risk include ideology, social unrest, changes in government due to political independence, the demands of local interest groups, internal political instability and international alliances. The risk factors become generalized through key actors: the government, the national legislature, opposition groups and foreign governments. The forms of political risk are diverse: confiscation, expropriation, operational restrictions, loss of transfer freedoms, contract cancellation, discriminatory application of host country law, and damage to physical plant or harm to employees.

Rood, L. L. "Nationalization and Indigenization in Africa." *Journal of Modern African Studies.* **14 (1976): 424-47.**

Focusing on pressures for local control, Rood reviews major African nationalizations and their effects on international law. Foreign ownership had completely dominated the economies of Black Africa. This was due, largely, to the nature of their colonial experience and the continuing role of expatriate technicians and managers. At independence, Black African economies had Europeans and Americans in key roles in major industries, Asians in the middle in wholesale or retail trade, and Africans at the bottom in farming and services.

Between 1950 and 1975, most large, extractive investments were nationalized. Small branches of multinational firms in banking, insurance and petroleum distribution were nationalized, and small- scale enterprises owned by resident aliens were indigenized. A listing of nationalizations is included.

Root, Franklin R. "The Expropriation Experience of American Companies." ***Business Horizons.*** **11 (April 1968): 69–74.**

In this pioneering article, Root reviews the expropriation experience of U.S. *Fortune 500* companies in the developing countries. Specific cases include the Soviet Union, Mexico, Eastern Europe, Cuba, Argentina, and Indonesia. Root surveyed executives of 38 American companies that had experienced expropriation with a mail questionnaire and follow-up interviews during 1966. A thirty-two percent return rate (106 replies) was accomplished on the mail questionnaire with 18 in-depth interviews realized.

Root details the expropriation sequence as seen by U.S. managers. The first step is a warning time before the expropriation takes place. This is followed by management response to that warning, expropriation, bargaining over compensation, and the postnationalization response of management to doing business in the former host country. Root called for the development of "political risk assessment" when that was a novel idea. "International executives are well advised to appraise the risk of expropriation (as well as other political risks) in an explicit, systematic fashion before committing resources to a foreign country." (p. 74).

Based on this survey, Root concluded that 187 U.S. companies had overseas affiliates that had been nationalized since World War II in 240 separate actions. Communist countries had taken affiliates of 171 firms; affiliates of 69 U.S. companies had been taken in non-communist countries. 137 U.S. based firms had lost direct investments in the massive Cuban nationalizations of 1959–60.

Root, Franklin R. "Foreign Government Constraints on U.S. Business Abroad." *Temple University Economic and Business Bulletin.* **20(1), (September 1967).**

Root develops a composite frequency index derived from responses by U.S. executives to a survey on perceptions of foreign political risk. The results of this 1966 survey provide a rank ordering of risk from the point of view of companies that had experienced nationalization. The ranking is: hostile officials (8.7 score), poor patent protection (8.3), high taxes (7.7), controls on prices (6.8), restrictions on personnel (6.8), restrictions on the repatriation of profit and capital (5.6), demands of the host government for equity participation (5.0), and restrictions on imports of raw materials (4.4).

Root, Franklin R., and Ahmed A. Ahmed. "The Influence of Policy Instruments on Manufacturing Direct Foreign Investments in Developing Countries." *Journal of International Business Studies.* **9(3), (Winter 1978): 81-93; and, "Empirical Determinants of Manufacturing Direct Foreign Investment in Developing Countries."** *Economic Development and Cultural Change.* **27 (July 1979): 751-67.**

Forty-one developing countries were analyzed with 44 variables measuring economic, social, political and policy conditions that were believed to affect the flow of foreign direct manufacturing investment (1966-70 per capita flow). Six variables were key: GDP per capita; the corporate tax level; the ratio of exports to imports; urbanization; infrastructure development; and regular executive transfers. The authors conclude that host country policies have small effects on investor behavior compared to the effects of market size and conditions.

St. Pierre, Maurice. "Race, Political Factors and the Nationalization of Demarara Bauxite Company, Guyana." *Social and Economic Studies.* **(1975): 481-503.**

The author provides a "sociological analysis of the dynamics of social change which led to the nationalization of Demba." (p. 481). The significance of the nationalization of Demba derives from the scale of the company's activity in Guyana, the overall size of the parent company (ALCAN, Ltd.), the demonstration effects throughout the Caribbean of this assertion of local control, and the elimination of colonial forms of control that had existed since independence.

Factors leading to the nationalization of Demba included the racial basis of the company's labor force, the exclusion of Guyanese from management positions, and the development of local institutions (e.g. the Guyana Mineworkers Union) that pressed for a larger share in decision-making.

Sauvant, Karl P., and Farid G. Lavipour (eds.). *Controlling Multinational Enterprise.* **Boulder: Westview Press, 1976, p. 335.**

This collection of independent works was compiled by the editors along with their work on an annotated bibliography on multinational corporations. Articles by recognized experts cover such topics as nationalizations in Guyana, the role of foreign direct investment in Nigeria, multinationals in East-West relations, the entry provisions of the Andean Common Market (ANCOM) countries, and the development of OPEC. The articles are supplemented by an extensive bibliography and statistical annexes.

Schreiber, Anna P. "Economic Coercion as an Instrument of Foreign Policy: U.S. Economic Measures Against Cuba and the Dominican Republic." ***World Politics.*** **25(3), (April 1973): 387-413.**

Schreiber reviews the history and effectiveness of U.S. economic coercion against Cuba from June 1960 and the Dominican Republic during 1960-62. The overthrow of Castro was the goal of U.S. policy that was responding to communist expansion, the role of the Soviet Union in Latin America and the expropriation of U.S companies. The objective of U.S. policy in the Dominican Republic was a response to lessons learned in Cuba. The goal was to force an end to the Trujillo regime before a Castro style revolution would occur. Schreiber concludes that economic coercion is most effective when accompanied by diplomatic and military initiatives.

Seidman, Ann, and Neva Seidman. ***South Africa and U.S. Multinational Corporations.*** **Westport, CT: Lawrence Hill and Company, 1977, p. 251.**

The authors' main themes are the increasing penetration of the South African economy by U.S. multinationals (over 400 subsidiaries as of 1977) and the growing industrialization of the economy in the midst of poverty for much of the black population. This book, originally published in Dar es Salaam, is a radical critique that takes South Africa's policy of *apartheid* as its point of departure. The authors provide historical analyses of the development of apartheid, the growth of the mining industry and the expansion of parastatal corporations. The analytic structure is Marxist: poverty leads to a lack of demand which leads to excessive military spending to absorb surplus production.

Shafer, Michael. "Capturing the Mineral Multinationals: Advantage or Disadvantage?" *International Organization.* **37(1), (Winter 1983): 93-119.**

On the basis of natural resource nationalizations, Shafer concludes that the loss of insulation from the world economy that comes with the expropriation of the foreign firm has negative effects on all Third World countries. These negative effects can be mitigated, however, in countries with a highly developed political system and strong state institutions. The success of nationalization can only be measured against its goals. Major goals discussed by Shafer include changing the distribution of wealth; the rationalization of economic planning, increasing government revenues in the host country, the indigenization of management positions and the silencing of domestic critics by taking over symbols of foreign exploitation.

In the two cases examined in detail (Zaire and Zambia), the promise of nationalization remained unfulfilled. Declines in the level and stability of the price of copper, labor unrest, mounting international debt, idle plants and declining investment have all eliminated the expected benefits of asserting local control. "Nationalization had unanticipated costs that either nullified its benefits or actually turned it against the interests of the nationalizers." Nationalization of the foreign investor removes the insulation that protected weak, developing economies from international change, the dilution of the copper market, the lack of indigenous talent and the disruptive effects of the struggle against Rhodesia.

Sigmund, Paul E. *Multinationals in Latin America: The Politics of Nationalization.* **Madison: University of Wisconsin Press, 1980, p. 426.**

Sigmund provides an overview of the international debate on the causes, effects and legal of nationationalization of foreign direct investment. National-level control of foreign business entry is described as a key element in the New International Economic Order. With the exception of Cuba, in the extractive, banking and utilities sectors, some compensation for nationalized property was paid investors. Sigmund attributes the high rate of nationalization in Latin America to domestic political pressures, the de-coupling of economic policies from the Cold War, and the expansion of host government capacity. General arguments are applied to four case studies: Cuba, Chile, Peru, and Venezuela.

Sklar, Richard L. *Corporate Power in an African State: The Political Impact of Multinational Mining Companies in Zambia.* **Berkeley: University of California Press, 1975, p. 245.**

Appointed a Senior Lecturer in Political Science at the University of Zambia in 1966, Sklar was uniquely positioned to observe and analyze the Zambianization of the copper industry. This exercise in political economy examines the history of Anglo-American and Roan Selection Trust in Zambia, the growth of the industry and the division of the benefits resulting from the traditional concession. Pressures for change in this relationship are attributed by Sklar to the rise of a skilled labor class, unionization, and urbanization around the Copperbelt.

Smith, P. S. "Bolivian Oil and Brazilian Economic Nationalism." *Journal of Inter-American Studies.* **12 (1971): 166-93.**

Smith provides a history of the development of Brazilian and Bolivian oil. He focuses on Brazil's failure to develop its oil concession in Bolivia's Chaco region. Originally rebuffed by Bolivia's economic nationalists, Brazil's Chaco venture foundered on Brazilian nationalism.

The discovery of oil in Brazil one year after the signing of the Chaco concession and the subsequent channeling of capital into Petrobras were responsible for choking off this international venture.

Solberg, Carl E. ***Oil and Nationalism in Argentina.*** **Stanford: Stanford University Press, 1979, p. 245.**

Solberg argues that the growth of state-owned oil companies in the Third World is due to the widely-held belief that rapid and sustained economic growth is impossible without national ownership of oil resources. *Yacimientos Petroliferos Fiscales* was the first, vertically-integrated, state-owned oil company outside of the Soviet Union. Solberg provides a history of YFP including its effects on Argentine economic development, international transactions and domestic political development.

Stoever, William A. "Endowments, Priorities and Policies: An Analytic Scheme for the Formulation of Developing Country Policy Toward Foreign Investment." *Columbia Journal of World Business.* **17(3), (Fall 1982): 3-15.**

Stoever's analytic scheme has three components: country endowments, priorities and policies. Endowments include natural resources, infrastructure, industrial base, population characteristics, proximity to markets, ties to capital exporting nations, tourism, attitudes toward foreign direct investment, governmental administrative resources and efficiency and its political stability.

Country priorities can include stimulating economic growth, capital formation, improving the balance of payments, enhancing government revenues, transferring technology, training local personnel, employment creation, and redistribution of income and wealth. Stoever suggestions the application of the principle of *triage* to these objectives, distinguishing those that are easy or hopeless to attain and those for which government intervention is crucial.

Policy levers at the disposal of the state include the investment climate, the efficiency of the administrative process (red tape), the selectivity of incentive structures, investment guarantees, the export-import balance, sources of financing and local ownership requirements.

Stoever, William A. "Renegotiations: The Cutting Edge of Relations Between MNCs and LDCs." *Columbia Journal of World Business.* **14(1), (Spring 1979): 5-14.**

Renegotiation often prompts a response of fear and anger on the part of multinational management but an analysis of three cases indicates that the results may not be as drastic as feared. These cases are Zambian copper, ITT in Chile and an unnamed manufacturing company in Peru. The case studies focus on the factors that cause a demand for renegotiating a contract, the appropriateness of the response of multinationals, and the types of changes which result. Renegotiation demands often result from changes in government, polarization of local politics, conspicuousness of the foreign-owned project and actions taken by the multinational itself or its home government.

Swansborough, Robert H. *The Embattled Colossus: Economic Nationalism and United States Investors in Latin America.* **Gainesville: University Presses of Florida, 1976, p. 261, and, "The American**

Investor's View of Latin American Economic Nationalism." *Inter-American Economic Affairs.* **26 (Winter 1972).**

Swansborough presents a history of major nationalizations in Latin America involving American investors (Cuba, Chile, Mexico and Peru). The central concern of this study is to track U.S. executives' views of foreign political risk and U.S. governmental initiatives to deal with it. The Council of the Americas sponsored a survey in 1970 to ascertain the attitudes of U.S. corporate managers on thes issues. A forty-eight percent response rate generated usable questionnaires from 100 firms accounting for 85 percent of U.S. foreign direct investment in the region.

Corporate managers stated that the issues of greatest concern to them were (1) restrictive economic policies; and, (2) political instability. They were more concerned in 1970 with administrative or regulatory changes than they were with formal expropriation. They often saw themselves as scapegoats for the failure of Latin American governments to solve their countries own economic problems. The size, historical dominance and sectoral concentration of much of U.S. direct investment made the multinationals a logical target of host government initiatives.

Torri, Michelguglielmo. "Factional Politics and Economic Policy: The Case of India's Bank Nationalization." *Asian Survey.* **15 (December 1975): 1077-97.**

Torri narrates the history of politics internal to the Congress Party up to the nationalizations. The 1967 national election was a debacle for the Congress Party. Accordingly, Indira Gandhi turned to the left in order to build support within the party and the electorate at large. The

Congress Party adopted a radical ten point program the first point of which was social control over the banking industry. Torri sees this as a tactic directed against the leadership of Morarji Desai. Negative aspects of banking behavior included declining credits for agriculture and low rate loans for insiders. After nationalization, the banks expanded their loans to farmers and eased credit terms. This resulted in a substantial increase in the base of support for the Congress Party in general and Indira Gandhi in particular.

Truitt, J. Frederick. ***Expropriation of Private Foreign Investment*** **Bloomington: University of Indiana Press, 1974, p. 164, and , "Expropriation of Foreign Investment: Summary of Post-World War II Experiences of American and British Investors in the Less Developed Countries."** ***Journal of International Business Studies.*** **1 (Autumn 1970): 21-34.**

Truitt's study is one of the first to apply explicit analytic constructs to the study of political risk. Expropriation policies in Algeria, Argentina, Brazil, Burma, Sri Lanka, India, Iraq, Nigeria, Syria, Tanzania and Egypt are catalogued and analyzed in order to identify factors in the host country and in the foreign investors themselves that effect the likelihood of expropriation. All economic sectors were included in this study of 40 British and 14 U.S. firms expropriated between 1945 and 1969. The data were collected from public sources, newspaper reports, and company documents. In addition to reports of expropriation, quantitative data and qualitative judgments are assembled on the characteristics of the host country (development, elite ideology, political stability, colonial heritage, international financial position, public sector-private sector mix) and of the firms that were expropriated (sector, size, dominance, effect on foreign exchange earnings, ownership, management practices).

The relative importance of these factors was evaluated quantitatively with percentage tables, matrices and checklists, and qualitatively with narratives about the context within which expropriations took place. Four variables were determined to have the greatest impact on the propensity to expropriate: internal political crises, the presence of communist trade or aid organizations within the host country, the vulnerability of the foreign firm to the loss of its assets in country, and the firm's impact on the host country's foreign exchange balances.

The generalizability of this analysis is limited because of the small number of countries covered, the aggregation of all industrial sectors, the absence of formal statistical tests of association and significance, and the lack of comparable data about other countries that, during this time period, chose not to expropriate foreign investment. Truitt's work is a rich source of hypotheses about the causes of political risk and, as an early work, broke important ground in data collection and evaluation.

Tugwell, Franklin. *The Politics of Oil in Venezuela.* **Stanford: Stanford University Press, 1975, p. 210.**

Tugwell reviews the history of Venezuelan petroleum policy between 1958 and 1975 on the basis of extensive interviews with local government officials and politicians. He focuses on the strategy adopted by the Venezuelan leadership in defining petroleum objectives, efforts by the multinationals to defend their profits and retain access to the crude oil, and the effects of the oil industry on Venezuelan development. Three factors are key to explaining the pattern of government–company relations in this sector: the role of ideology in setting out alternative policies; the impact of domestic political developments; and, the movement of Venezuelan policymakers and politicians along a learning curve, thereby increasing their bargaining power.

Tugwell argues the interdependence of domestic politics and oil policy. National political life in Venezuela is characterized as moderately mobilized. Elections are fair and competitive. The stake of these elections was increasing over time as the role of the state in national economic life increased. With the electoral victory of Betancourt in 1958, a new generation of political leaders came to the fore.

Walters, Kenneth D., and R. Joseph Monsen. "The Spreading Nationalization of European Industry." ***Columbia Journal of World Business.*** **16(4), (Winter 1981): 62-72.**

Traditionally, state-owned enterprises had operated in the transportation, utilities and infrastructure sectors of the West European economies. During the 1970s state-owned firms expanded in pharmaceuticals, electronics, computers, office equipment, petroleum, microelectronics, pulp and paper and telecommunications. This expansion was the results of desires to rescue declining industries, to support high-risk ventures that would not otherwise be undertaken, assert control over national resources (oil), or for reasons of political philosophy.

In France during 1970s, state companies diversified nationally and internationally into new sectors and geographic regions. Under the socialist government of Mitterand, direct nationalization of French and foreign-owned firms took place. In the U.K. nationalization was primarily a defensive weapon for the rescuing of ailing industries (Rolls-Royce and British Leyland) and the preservation of jobs. Walters also reviews the growth of state enterprises in Italy, West Germany, Norway, Austria and Sweden.

Wallace, Brian F. "Multinational Corporations and Governments in Developing Nations: Effects on the Distribution of Wealth and Power in Colombia." *Paper Presented at the Annual Meeting of the International Studies Association.* **(Philadelphia: March 18-21, 1981), p. 37.**

Wallace contrasts the performance and effects of foreign owned and national manufacturing plants. He includes 421 foreign-owned firms in Colombia between 1970 and 1974 and compares them to approximately 6,066 national firms employing more than ten people. Local ownership (public or private) is an alternative to foreign ownership. Colombia has announced indigenization as one of its national objectives in the area of investment management. Given the other goals of Colombian policy, Wallace examines the extent to which ownership effects behavior.

In twenty-three of twenty-seven industrial groups foreign firms paid higher salaries than their Colombian counterparts. This finding is supported by evidence from cross-national studies undertaken by the International Labor Organization. Foreign firms are less likely to stimulate employment than national firms. The capital intensity of foreign firms is much higher than that of nationally-owned firms. While capital intensity is detrimental to job creation, it is instrumental to another Colombian goal - technology transfer. Foreign plants are more concentrated geographically than are national firms. Foreigners tend to congregate in the major cities. Overall, however, Wallace observed more similarities than differences in his empirical comparison of foreign and Colombian firms.

Williams, M.L. "Extent and Significance of Nationalization of Foreign-Owned Assets in Developing Countries, 1956-72." *Oxford Economic Papers.* **27 (July 1975): 260-73.**

Williams develops a measure of the extent of nationalization of foreign investment in forty developing countries over the period 1956-72. This proportional measure includes all sectors of the economy. The index is derived from public sources on nationalizations and OECD data on investment flows and stocks. The denominator of Williams' ratio is the stock of foreign direct investment outstanding in 1972. This measure is based on the OECD's estimate of 1967 book values with projections made by Williams up to 1972. The numerator of the ratio is the estimated value of all nationalizations after estimated compensation payments have been made. Data are presented in terms of two coefficients: a proportional measure of nationalization and a confiscation coefficient.

Williams classifies host countries according to the proportion of investment nationalized. Socialist countries are those taking more than 80 percent within this time period. These countries are Cuba, Chile, Burma, Egypt, Iraq, Syria and Bangladesh. The distribution of nationalization coefficients is shown by country, time and sector. Vulnerable sectors were mining, utilities and petroleum. Williams also presents evidence in support of the diffusion hypothesis.

Wu, F.W. "The Political Risk of Foreign Direct Investment in Post-Mao China: A Preliminary Assessment." *Management International Review.* **22(1), (1982): 13-25.**

Foreign direct investment is one element in China's current modernization program. Wu analyzes the Chinese investment climate from the point of view of political risk facing the foreign company. Factors relevant to this assessment for China include: leadership stability, socialist ideology vs. capitalist principles, and centralization vs. decentralization of economic decision-making in post-Mao China. Wu considers China to be a moderately low-risk country. Information on the political risk industry is also presented.

Walter, John P. "U.S. Foreign Investment Expropriations in Latin America, 1903-78." *Journal of Energy and Development.* **5(1), (Autumn 1979): 107-22.**

The causes of expropriation are analyzed, techniques for reducing risk are suggested, and potential differences in Latin American business climates are evaluated. A list of disputes is presented based on State Department and other public sources. Five major causes of risk in the resource area, according to Walter, were (1) disagreements in principle over the legality of resource ownership by foreign firms, (2) ideological differences, (3) political motivations of host country political leaders, (4) unacceptable behavior by the foreign firms, and, (5) specific contract problems.

Walters, Kenneth. D. "Nationalized Firm - Politician's Free Lunch." *Columbia Journal of World Business.* **12(1), (Spring 1977): 90-102.**

Based on a review of national companies in Western Europe, Walters concludes that the social and political benefits of state ownership do not justify the economic costs, except for local politicians. National companies are used to build political support through boosted employment, stable prices and honoring of promises to labor unions.

The financial performance of state companies has been poor. This is true not only of British companies, but those on the continent as well. Walters attributes this poor performance to several factors. Many state companies were on the verge of bankruptcy when they were taken over. These bailouts were, in many cases, structurally inefficient. An improvement in aggregate demand would not rescue moribund smokestack industries. Many firms were nationalized for ideological reasons without regard for the balance sheet. Government interference with the management of national companies has exacerbated an already difficult situation.

Recommendations for managing the national firm include: making goals clear, requiring the government to make direct and explicit payments for the social goals levied on firms, recruiting and retaining able management, a non-ideological board of directors committed to financial solvency, insulation of management from political pressures, promoting competition between nationalized firms, and adopting rational financial policies.

Yoffie, David B. "The Newly Industrializing Countries and the Political Economy of Protectionism." ***International Studies Quarterly.*** **25(4), (December 1981): 569-600.**

Yoffie begins with a statement of a paradox in international relations: weak actors often prevail over ones that are stronger in objective, material terms. The newly industrializing countries (NICS) can turn protectionism to their advantage by emphasizing bargaining rather than coercion. The new form of protectionism (voluntary quotas) has replaced rigid mandatory quotas and tariffs, opening the way for bargaining by developing countries. This bargaining process can have substantial payoffs for multinationals that export from the Third World to the industrial states.

Yoffie advises the NICs to adopt a bargaining strategy that will avoid political confrontations, will allow for export diversification, avoid overspecialization, maintain linkages to other policy areas and achieve flexibility through ambiguity. Such a strategy is based on the view that the protectionist game is a political one and that with sectoral compromises, NICs can maintain their access to broad markets. In the event of voluntary quotas being accepted, NICs can trade up by selling a smaller number of a higher quality product.

Zink, Dolph Warren. ***The Political Risks for Multinational Enterprise in Developing Countries: With a Case Study of Peru.*** **New York: Praeger Publishers, 1973, p. 185.**

This is an early study of the growing political risks faced by multinationals in countries at traditional levels of development. Zink based his analysis of political risk on the case study of Peru and structured interviews at 187 U.S. corporations accounting for 80 percent of all U.S. outward foreign direct investment. Zink began with the notion that "there exists within political science a body of knowledge that would be useful to international business and that there is a gap in the literature bridging the two disciplines" (p. vii). Zink provides an historical overview of multinationals in the Third World, discusses the sources of political risk, and reviews the interaction of governments and businesses. He provides an outlook for risk in Peru that was based on an analysis of the various power groups in that country: government, Indians, middle class, clergy, the military and political parties.

Interviews with corporate executives revealed the parlous state of political risk analysis. Only 9 percent of the companies employed a full-time political analyst. Only one-third conducted political forecasting on a continuing basis. Less than 10 percent used outside political consultants. Roughly half had established a procedure for feeding political judgments into corporate decision-making. When asked about sources of information on political risk, country managers (79 percent) and general news sources (61 percent) received high marks. Banks and U.S. government agencies were cited by substantial numbers of firms interviewed (56 and 43 percent, respectively). A corporation's internal political staff was cited as an important source by only one-fourth of the corporate executives. For a comparison of Zink's findings to a more recent study by the Conference Board see Kobrin (1982).

Chapter Four: Analyzing and Managing Political Risk

Van Agtmael, Antoine. "How Business Has Dealt with Political Risk." *Financial Executive.* **(January 1976): 26-30.**

Political risk in the Third World is defined. Nationalization or expropriation of investment is cited as the greatest risk facing foreign investors. The author suggests ways that multinationals can anticipate risk, prepare for its consequences and continue to function effectively in an unstable environment. A small proportion of U.S. owned companies actually lend, sell or invest overseas. Among those that are active in the Third World, few conduct sophisticated political risk assessments before venturing overseas. Types of risk and their relation to the business are seldom specified. Few firms make an explicit trade-off between risk and return. Once the commitment is made, there is little in the way of continuing tracking of the environment. Generally, corporate managers have low levels of political skills. The author attributes this situation to the uneasiness with which traditional managers regard analytic methods, databases and computers in general. Compared to economic analysis, political assessment lacks a general theory, a convincing analytic model, and timely, relevant data.

Van Agtmael suggests a checklist for assessing political risk. Although this is qualitative, it does provide some rigor to the process. Key factors in this checklist are: time and mode of national independence, record of stability, sense of national unity, ethno-linguistic diversity, opposition parties, corruption, voting trends, government responsiveness to the needs of the population, role of the military, sources of potential unrest, and external economic and political factors.

Aharoni, Yair. ***The Foreign Investment Decision Process.*** **Boston: Harvard University, Graduate School of Business, 1966, p. 362.**

This classic analysis of the investment decision process is a revised version of a doctoral dissertation submitted to the Harvard Business School. Distressed over the low level of U.S. foreign direct investment in developing countries , Aharoni undertook in 1960 research on how major U.S. companies made foreign investment decisions. The focus was on firms that had invested in Israel. There are five phases to that decision process. The first is the decision to look abroad. The second is the investigation of investment opportunities. The third is the decision itself. The fourth is reviews and negotiations within the firm. The last step is an analysis of the social situation and risks facing the investment. It is instructive that, in Aharoni's research, U.S. companies undertook risk assessment after the fact.

Aharoni's research undercut the conventional wisdom concerning investment decisionmaking. First, the corporation is not a single, decisionmaking unit. Like the nation-state, large companies are composed of many bureaucratic entities, each of which may have a different perspective on a given investment. Similarly, the corporation does not have a single and known set of utility preferences. Tensions between loan officers and credit officers are only the most cited instance of opposing roles within major banks and, by extension, multinational companies. Corporate decisionmakers also will not know the full range of alternatives and the consequences of each. Lastly, they will be unable, in most instances, to calculate the expected utility of each alternative. These findings indicate that corporate decisions are made in an environment characterized by imperfect information, uncertainty and bargaining within the organization.

Allen, Michael R., and W. Kip Viscusi. "Insuring Expropriation Risk of Multinational Firms." ***Stanford Journal of International Studies.*** **11 (Spring 1976): 153-68.**

Allen and Viscusi argue that the increase (during the late 1960s and 1970s) in extent of expropriation poses serious financial risks for multinational corporations. In a perfect world, insurance could be purchased to offset expropriation risk. However, the market for political risk insurance is imperfect and, for many capital-exporting countries, subject to complex government requirements. Allen and Viscusi review the legal options available to expropriated firms, basic insurance concepts and incentives to insure against political risk, and the coverage available through private and public risk insurers. The distinguishing feature of expropriation risk is that, according to these authors, its assessment is based on subjective judgments, not actuarial data as in the case of life insurance.

Anon. "Harsh Lessons of Iran." ***Executive.*** **22(6), (June 1980): 46-8.**

Canadian firms are advised to be more aware of the political and social conditions that can affect their operations abroad. The need for political consultants has yet to be fully recognized by Canadian firms. Political risk insurance, through public or private underwriters, does not eliminate the need for political analysis. Some countries are uninsurable. In the absence of a sound country assessment, a multinational might be over-insured. Lack of information about the real risks will lead to missed opportunities.

Anon. "Intelligence on the Real World." *Executive.* **22(6), (June 1980): 49-50.**

This short article describes the activities of Benjamin Weiner, a former U.S. Department of State official, who founded his own political risk business in 1970: Probe International, Inc. According to Weiner, there is no such thing as a "safe" country. Multinational firms have to anticipate adverse political developments and cope with them, not run from them. Weiner's approach is based on personal visits to countries under analysis and contacts with policymakers and other elites.

Apter, David E., and Louis Wolf Goodman (eds.). *The Multinational Corporation and Social Change.* **New York: Praeger Publishers, 1976, p. 234.**

This edited collection is based on a conference held at Yale University during 1974 at the Institution for Social and Policy Studies. Articles by Apter and Vernon present the liberal interpretation of the role of multinational corporations in the international economy and discuss the effects of multinationalization on the shrinkage of international space and development prospects within the Third World. The authors realize, that, despite their putative effects on welfare, multinational corporations have an impact on host societies that varies across social classes. Goodman examines the social basis of decision-making in multinational corporations and presents findings based on interviews with corporate managers. Other topics covered in this collection are the effects of MNCs on development, the expansion of Japanese-based MNCs into Asia and the effect of MNCs on OECD international trade.

Ascher, William. ***Forecasting: An Appraisal for Policy Makers and Planners.*** **Baltimore: Johns Hopkins University Press, 1979, p. 239.**

This study on forecasting is directed to planners and analysts who need to make or at least consume forecasts in their everyday work. Ascher reviews problems of forecasting and the impact of expert forecasts in the corporate and government sectors. Specific types of forecasts are analyzed: population, macroeconomic, energy, transportation and technology. Ascher emphasizes the importance to the final result of core assumptions, the interconnectedness of forecasting tasks, and the nascent state of social or political forecasting. Social and political forecasting may be stillborn because of its "unappraisability." Vague forecasts are characteristic of much social or political analysis. As such, the accuracy of the forecasts cannot be ascertained and the methodology cannot advance.

Baade, Hans. "Indonesian Nationalization Measures Before Foreign Courts: A Reply." *American Journal of International Law.* **54 (October 1960): 801-35.**

This is a Reply to Martin Domke concerning the ruling of the West German courts on the effects of Indonesian nationalization measures on goods and securities situated in West Germany. West German courts were caught between violations of international law from the perspectives of either Indonesia or the Netherlands. Baade reviews public international law on expropriation, compensation, and claims procedures.

Baglini, N. A. "Political Risk", *National Underwriter - Property and Casualty Insurance.* **86(51) (December 17, 1982): pp. 16-20**

This articles reviews corporate strategies for offsetting political risk. These include use of a local partner, local borrowing, and political risk insurance provided by public and private underwriters. Two investment sectors have been particularly vulnerable to risk. These are foreign investors in the natural resource extraction sector and those operating in the basic and financial infrastructures: transportation, utilities, banking and insurance.

Bailey, Katherine C. "Profiling an Effective Risk Assessment Team." ***Risk Management.*** **30(2) (February 1983): 34-38.**

Bailey reviews corporate efforts to develop methods for analyzing the political risks involved in doing business in the Third World. The risk assessment team has been found to be the best method for this type of analysis. A risk assessment team consists of individuals with management skills, knowledge of the area or country, and social science research skills. A methodology for political risk assessment is presented.

Bannister, J. "Does the Risk Manager Have A Role in Handling Political Risk?" ***Risk Management*** **28(10) (October 1981): 98-102.**

The effects of political risk are often accentuated by management problems within the firm. Local managers can act to reduce the negative effects of host country action in several ways. These include the building of public support within the community (being a good corporate citizen), learning more about the political environment and attitudes toward business in your part of the world, and establish as far as possible the rules of the game at the outset of your activities in country.

Betts, Richard K. "Analysis, War and Decision: Why Intelligence Failures are Inevitable." ***World Politics.*** **31(1), (October 1978): 61-89.**

The core of the intelligence process is the acquisition, analysis and appreciation of relevant data (p. 61). Betts argues that failure should be put into perspective. What are the success rates of alternative forecasting organizations or methods? Indeed, the successes of the intelligence community are seldom mentioned. Their failures are painfully discussed in the public domain. Intelligence production and intelligence consumption are two different problems. More and better intelligence production is not sufficient for effective decisionmaking in foreign affairs. Although the intelligence analyst is not responsible for the use to which his product is put, intelligence is often judged by the quality of decisionmaking throughout the executive branch.

Barriers to analytic accuracy include the ambiguity of evidence, the ambivalence of judgment (on the one hand...), and the atrophy of reforms within the intelligence bureaucracy. Solutions are evasive. Betts reviews the strengths and weaknesses of several putative solutions to America's intelligence "failures". These are (1) assume the worst; (2) multiple advocacy; (3) consolidation of collection and reporting; (4) use of devil's advocates; (5) sanctions and incentives; and, (6) cognitive rehabilitation and methodological consciousness on the part of consumers (how do we know type questions).

Blake, David H. ***Managing the External Relations of Multinational Corporations.*** **New York: Fund for Multinational Management Education, 1977, p. 100.**

The public affairs function of major U.S. multinationals is examined through interviews conducted during 1975–76 with executives from 40 corporations. The theme of the book is "relationship management" – the sensitizing of the corporation to the environment, the integration of the public affairs function with other management functions, and the development of a systematic approach to public affairs. The danger to effective public relations, particularly in unfamiliar political situations, is to never get beyond the fires in the in-basket.

Corporate managers are alerted to the possible political and social effects of multinational activity, particularly in the developing world, in order to assess the likely concerns of the host country. Blake discusses how the public affairs function can be integrated into management, made a part of the planning process, and increase the flow of relevant information within and outside the corporation.

Blank, Stephen, Joseph LaPalombara and Paul M. Sacks. *Political Analysis and Forecasting in the Private Sector: An Overview of the New Firm-Centric Analytic Formats.* **New York: Conference Board, August 1980, p. 54.**

The authors review the development of the political risk industry during the late 1970s. The original data on corporate risk assessment practices were gathered through a mailed questionnaire and selected follow-up interviews. The factors that prompted the emergence of private sector political analysis and the nature of individual corporate response are discussed.

The survey material is supplemented by detailed case studies of risk assessment techniques used by Shell (ASPRO), Getty, World Political

Risk Forecasts (a Frost and Sullivan product), Mathtech and the Futures Group. These reviews give the reader insight into both internal (Shell and Getty) and external approaches to risk assessment.

Overall the authors conclude that the use of expert panels and subjective assessments are more common than quantitative techniques or formal modeling in those firms where risk assessment has been institutionalized at all. The authors conclude that European-based multinationals are better able to cope with political risk than their American counterparts. This greater ease with political developments is due to the Europeans' longer experience with developing countries during the colonial period, the greater (on average) cosmopolitanism of West European managers, and the longer duration of foreign assignments for European managers.

Blank, Stephen, with John Basek, and Stephen J. Kobrin. *Assessing the Political Environment: An Emerging Function in International Companies.* **New York: Conference Board, 1981, p. 72.**

This assessment by the Conference Board examines two key questions: How do American corporations define non-economic factors (political risk)? and, How is this definition related to characteristics of the company (size, sector, internationalization)? Written questionnaires were mailed to CEOs of 435 firms. Usable replies were received back from 193 (43 percent). A subsample of forty firms was drawn and interviews were held with 115 executives from thirty-seven of these.

The authors conclude that corporate awareness of the relevance and importance of political risk is growing. Most corporations lack a model of environmental effects on business that would be useful, minimally, to establish information collection categories and priorities. Little progress has been made in information standardization that would support comparison across countries. Systems are lacking for the assessment of information quality and the testing of analytic forecasts. Overall, political risk assessment in major American multinationals and banks remains unsystematic, ad hoc and judgmental.

Bocksteigel, Karl-Heinz. "Arbitration of Disputes Between States and Private Enterprises in the International Chamber of Commerce." *American Journal of International Law.* **59 (July 1965): 579-86.**

Bocksteigel reviews existing practices of commercial arbitration as undertaken by the International Chamber of Commerce in Paris, disputes settled by the ICC and the advantages of ICC arbitration.

Bradley, David G. "Managing Against Expropriation." *Harvard Business Review.* **(July-August 1977): 75-83.**

Bradley bases this analysis of expropriation on information from the Harvard Multinational Enterprise Project and the U.S. Department of State. Harvard reported 114 nationalizations among the 16,000 foreign affiliates in its database on U.S.-owned manufacturing companies. The State Department reported approximately 260 takings in all economic sectors. Bradley concluded that expropriation could not be avoided through generic solutions like general political analysis or restructuring equity through joint ventures. Risk analysis should be firm specific. Vulnerability is affected by ownership, technology, vertical integration, size and project characteristics. Vulnerability varies by sector with firms in extractive industries and banking more vulnerable than manufacturing enterprises. Bradley also notes the importance of diffusion in assessing political risk. International learning effects were apparent in the case of African banks in 1970, Latin American utilities in 1971 and Middle East oil companies after 1974.

Bradley develops a strategy to reduce risk. Joint ventures are recommended. The multinational should also concentrate proprietary research, product development and processing technology in the United States. Each new investment should be dependent economically (e.g. for sales) on the parent. Manufacturing should trade on brand recognition and avoid local branding in the host market. Finally, the foreign investor should adopt a low profile, preferably with a multi-plant strategy.

Brenner, Lynn. "How to Insure Against Political Risk." *Institutional Investor.* **15(4) (April 1981): 211-13.**

Corporate executives are increasingly aware of the political risks attendant to doing business overseas. The task of assessing those risks falls on the expanding political risk insurance field. Risk is project specific. That is, risk varies with host country, industry and firm. These factors must be evaluated in conjunction with the host country's political, social and economic condition. Strategies for offsetting risk, according to Brenner, include the use of local partners, integration with the parent firm, and close contact with local government officials. The political and social climate should be constantly monitored.

Brewer, Thomas L. "The Instability of Governments and the Instability of Controls on Fund Transfers by Multinational Enterprises: Implications for Political Risk Analysis." *Journal of International Business Studies* **14(3), (Winter 1983): 147-57.**

A spate of quantitative research on the causes of expropriation receives a much needed complement from Brewer's cross-national study on causes of the instability of fund transfers controls. Data were collected on 115 nations from 1970 to 1979. Transfer controls (profits, fees, royalties, interest, debt, and equity) were coded from the IMF's annual reports on control practices. This empirical study distinguishes governmental instability as one cause of political risk. The data support Brewer's hypotheses that:

(1) Governmental instability affects transfer policy,

(2) The effects are weak, and,

(3) They vary by type of governmental instability (personnel shifts, factional changes, and systemic changes).

Overall, the proportion of variance explained by these regression models is low; transfer policy changes were more successfully modelled for industrial countries compared to developing countries. This analysis indicates that economic, rather than political, factors are the driving forces behind instability in transfer policy.

Brewer, Thomas L. "Political Risk Assessment for Foreign Direct Investment Decision: Better Methods for Better Results." *Columbia Journal of World Business.* **16(1) (Spring 1981): 5-12.**

Brewer distinguishes several different forms of risk and the various sources of risk. Risk types include physical destruction, expropriation, currency convertibility, labor unrest, changes in taxes, tariffs and non-tariff barriers to trade. Four basic models of the political process are evaluated in terms of their relevance for assessing political risk.

These models are (1) state-centric approaches; (2) pluralist politics or interest group approaches; (3) bureaucratic politics or organizational behavior approaches; and, (4) transnational political explanations.

The complexity of political analysis calls for the collection and processing of diverse sorts of information. The results of that analysis should be incorporated early into the capital-budgeting process to have an effect on decision-making.

Bunn, D. W., and M. M. Mustafaoglu. "Forecasting Political Risk." *Management Science.* **(November 1978): pp. 1557-67.**

This paper presents a technique in practical application by an American oil company for forecasting political risks faced by its investments in developing countries. These risks include expropriation, discriminatory taxation, and operational controls on prices and production. The basic data inputs on factors leading to risk are provided by an expert panel of country and industry experts. Barjesian analysis is used to estimate probabilities of occurrence of political risk events. Cross-impact analysis generates alternative scenarios.

Carlston, Kenneth S. "Concession Agreements and Nationalization." *American Journal of International Law.* **52 (April 1958): 260-77.**

A concession agreement is a coordinating agreement between a government and a private firm allowing for the international development of economic resources. Carlston reviews the historical operation of concession agreements under an international legal system that tolerates expropriation. Cases of nationalized concessions are reviewed (Lena Goldfieds, Anglo-Iranian Oil). In an era characterized by multiple revolutions (technological, organizational, political), capitalist and socialist states need to adopt international concession agreements that will facilitate resource exploitation.

Choi, Frederick D. S. "Political Risk: An Accounting Challenge." *Management Accounting.* **60(12), (June 1979): 17-20.**

Political risk is defined as expropriation and restrictions on operating freedoms. The author reviews the elements of political risk and their implications for financial accounting. He argues for a systematic accounting approach to risk assessment. Following Knudsen, Choi proposes a database on national welfare and aspiration variables. A general ratio of aspiration to welfare would be used as an indicator of nations heading into trouble. Choi also argues for the use of internal accounting measures to evaluate costs and benefits of strategies to offset risk: joint ventures, local sourcing, etc.

Chamberlain, Neil W. "Managerial Responses to Social Change in Western Europe." *Columbia Journal of World Business.* **13(4) (Winter 1978):31-38.**

Squeezed by increasing government intervention and a growing labor disaffection, managers are more concerned about their role and authority within the firm. Traditional management prerogatives (employment, plant location, choice of technology, expansion plans) are increasingly undermined by the activities of government ministries and labor representatives. The growing role of labor has been institutionalized through the placement of labor representatives on corporate boards (co- determination). Labor concerns over job security and working conditions form the basis for heightened involvement with other aspects of management. Chamberlain attributes much of the erosion of mangement prerogatives to egalitarianism rather than class consciousness and the declining performance of major West European industries.

Chevalier, A., and G. Hirsch. "The Assessment of the Political Risk in the Investment Decision." *Journal of the Operational Research Society.* **32(7) (July 1981): 599-610.**

The evaluation of political risk is an important element in international business. Chevalier and Hirsch define and explore the different aspects of political risk. Different approaches to the assessment of risk are presented. The integration of risk assessment into financial planning is considered. The authors suggest further research into the assessment of political risk and its incorporation into decision-making.

Coplin, William D., and Michael K. O'Leary. "Systematic Political Risk Analysis for Planners." *Planning Review.* **2(1) (January 1983): 14-17**

Corporate planners operating on a worldwide basis need to know about the political stability of the countries in which they are or will be operating. Political instability is one factor, among many, that generate risk for foreign businesses. Coplin and O'Leary describe the *World Political Risk Forecasts* prepared by Frost and Sullivan. These forecasts cover six month and five year forecasts based on political conditions, business and trade restrictions and other economic policies, including expropriation. Two tables are presented. One depicts how the risk factors are derived. The other presents country scores (letter grades) on the major components of risk.

Davies, W. "Unsticking the State of the Art of Political Risk Management." *Sloan Management Review.* **22(4) (Summer 1981): 59-63.**

Davies observes that the Iranian revolution and its torturous aftemath have heightened corporate sensitivity to the social and political exposure of foreign direct investments. He argues that the state of the art in risk assessment is stuck because of an inappropriate focus on country risk. Risk is a property of specfic firms, investments or projects. What concerns management is not the general political condition of the host country, but how changes in that environment will effect their firm. Davies proposes that management shift its attention from country to project risk.

Davies, W. "Beyond the Earthquake Allegory: Managing Political Risk Vulnerability." *Business Horizons.* **24(4), (July-August 1981): 39-43.**

Risk management is the essential companion to risk analysis. In the era of discriminatory expropriation, increasing government regulation and intervention, the identification and management of risks have become feasible objectives. Host countries have become more discerning in their policies toward foreign investors as they attempt to realize concrete commercial or political objectives. Widespread nationalizations undertaken for symbolic or ideological reasons have given way to selective actions which can be anticipated by foreign firms. Davies argues that risk can be best managed by regional or divisional managers rather than line executives operating in the host country.

Dolzer, R. "New Foundations of the Law of Expropriation of Alien Property." *American Journal of International Law.* **75(3), (1981): 553-89.**

This article is presented in a theme issue of the *American Journal of International Law* that focuses on the legal aspects of expropriation. Dolzer observes that most of the dialogue on expropriation has been political rather than legal in nature since 1973. That period was marked by the demise of the Hull principle (prompt, adequate and effective compensation) and the collapse of the Calvo doctrine (non-interference by the government of capital-exporting states). Sources of change in host country policy toward foreign investors are found in desires for self-determination and concern over the balance of payments.

Domke, Martin. "Indonesian Nationalization Measures Before Foreign Courts." *American Journal of International Law.* **54 (April 1960): 305-23.**

In 1958, the government of Indonesia nationalized the holdings of Dutch private citizens, including tobacco plantations. The 1958 harvest was exported to the Netherlands and West Germany and was claimed in local courts by the expropriated Dutch owners. Claims for relief were successful in the Netherlands but failed in West Germany. According to Domke, the West German court's acceptance of the "extraterritorial" nature of the Indonesian nationalizations was contrary to international law.

Donath, B. "Handicapping and Hedging the Foreign Investment." *Industrial Marketing.* **66(2), (February 1981): 56-61.**

Foreign direct investment involves risk from a number of sources. The most likely form of risk are changes in host government political or economic policies that will make the difference between a successful and an unsuccessful investment.

The Association of Political Risk Analysts (APRA) was formed in 1980 and counts approximately 125 corporate and 300 individual members. Its objective is to monitor the political climate in developing countries. Risk factors are presented. Suggestions for offsetting or reducing risk are given. Charts are included.

Eells, Richard. "Multinational Corporations: The Intelligence Function, " pp. 140-155 in Courtney Brown (ed.), ***World Business: Promises and Problems.*** **New York: Macmillan, 1970, p. 338.**

Intelligence is necessary if the enterprise is to survive and grow. Intelligence involves receiving messages from the environment, the integration of those messages with existing information, the use of that combined information to make decisions, and the communications of those decisions throughout the company. The content of corporate intelligence ranges from basic descriptive pieces (getting the facts straight) to current reporting to speculative or evaluative analysis. All three forms are essential. The last is most useful to corporate strategic planners and capital budgeters.

Eiteman, D. K. "Model for Expropriation Settlement: Peruvian-IPC Controversy." ***Business Horizons.*** **13(2), (April 1970): 85-91.**

Eiteman accepts political risk as a fact of doing business overseas. In the face of apparently inexorable efforts by Third World governments to nationalize key industries, how can compensation be determined according to traditional international legal standards? Simulations of commercial transactions at the time of takeover are inadequate. The Peruvian-IPC case displayed great differences in the claims and counter- claims made by both parties. IPC's claim for compensation in th amount of $170 million was reduced to $70 million by the government of Peru. These funds were blocked until IPC paid the $690 million in "illegal profits" that it had earned in Peru. It is precisely this situation of retroactive expropriation with compensation that Eiteman addresses. The solution presented is the present compound value of net cash flow between parent and subsidiary during the life of the investment with an assumed 15 percent compounding factor.

Ensor, Richard J (ed.). ***Assessing Country Risk.*** **London: Euromoney Publications, 1981, p. 172.**

This Euromoney publication is a handbook by practitioners on the data and methods used for analyzing the economic and political dimensions of country risk. The central concern is international financial exposure. Different techniques are used to assess creditworthiness by a wide variety banks and industrial firms. Specific techniques used by U.S. firms for analyzing political risk and offsetting such risk are presented. Factors that are included in a risk calculation are the country's resources, the policies of the government, its economic structure, its debt service ratio and the diversity of its export structure. This last measure is one method for gauging the country's longer-term flexibility in coping with changes in the international economy. Country risk assessments are used to set country limits, influence the interest rate, adjust the payback period and re-insurance of the loan or investment.

Fahey, Liam, and William R. King. "Environmental Scanning for Corporate Planning." ***Business Horizons.*** **20 (1977): 61-71.**

Information about the corporation's environment is emphasized in current thinking about long-term planning. Fahey and King describe the practice of environmental scanning underway in twelve large U.S. corporations. Most of the information used in such scanning is generated in the operating environment and through accumulation of general political, economic or social knowledge.

Three scanning approaches exist. Irregular scanning is ad hoc, crisis driven and seeks out the implications of recent events. Regular scanning is periodic (often annual) and is decision-oriented. Use of annual reports by major banks to set country limits is an example of regular scanning. Continuous scanning involves the monitoring of environmental systems (business, economics, politics, technology) by an organizationally-structured corporate scanning agency. Although the choice of a scanning method varied by industry, all firms perceived themselves as doing a poor job of environmental scanning.

Field, P. "Meet the New Breed of Banker." ***Euromoney.*** **(July 1980): 9-21.**

The new breed of banker is the political risk expert. Events in Iran, South Korea and Central America have stimulated U.S. banks to increase the internal resources they allocate to political and social analysis when they assess the risks of overseas lending.

Galtung, Johan. "On the Effects of International Economic Sanctions, With Examples from the Case of Rhodesia." *World Politics.* **19(3), (April 1967): 387-416.**

The purpose of sanctions is to punish an offending party or force compliance with the demands of the sanctioning party. Sanctions have both a negative and positive dimension. Galtung focuses on the psychological and social aspects of the economic boycott underway against Rhodesia at the time the article was written. The larger purpose of the essay is to define and describe sanctions as an international political weapon and assess the reasons for their (in)effectiveness.

Sanctions may be directed against the international communications of a target (blockade), the target's economy or its diplomatic relations. They may be negative (punishing) or positive (rewarding), individual or collective, internal to the target or external, unilateral or multilateral from the point of view of the sanctioning states, general or selective (e.g. blocking all trade or letting food and pharmaceuticals through), and total or partial.

Vulnerability to sanctions is a function of concentration of alternatives. Countries where the domestic economy is concentrated in a few key commodities, or that have an export structure oriented to a small number of consumers, or that export only a few commodities are much more vulnerable to economic sanctions than those countries that have diversified domestic and international economic structures. In general, however, sanctions are ineffective because they are diffidently applied and often promote internal political and social integration within the target country. Overall, public, economic and bilateral sanctions are a poor means of investment protection.

Gantz, David A. "The Marcona Settlement: New Forms of Negotiation and Compensation for Nationalized Property." *American Journal of International Law.* **71 (July 1977): 474-93.**

Gantz presents the history of Marcona in Peru, the context of the 1974 expropriation, the three phases of negotiations between the Peruvian and U.S. Governments, and the implications of the agreement for U.S. - Peruvian relations and U.S. expropriation policy. The negotiated compensation package was a cash payment and long-term sales relationship that was of benefit to both parties.

Gerowin, Mina. "U.S. Regulations of Foreign Direct Investment: Current Developments and the Congressional Response." *Virginia Journal of International Law.* **15 (Spring 1975): 611-47.**

Gerowin discusses growing concern about foreign direct investment *into* the United States, particularly investment by the Japanese. Inward foreign direct investment exceeded two billion dollars in 1973, spurring Congressional reconsideration of the traditional "Open Door" policy of the U.S. The issues, fear of economic dominance and the potential use of foreign investment as policy instruments by foreign governments, mirror earlier concerns in the Third World about direct investments originating in the industrial countries. Gerowin reviews alternative approaches to investment control (unilateral, bilateral and multilateral) and recommends the establishment at the federal level of an information collection and analysis organization before laws governing foreign investment are written.

Geyikdagi, Mehmet Yasar. *Risk Trends of U.S. Multinational and Domestic Firms.* **New York: Praeger Publishers, 1982, p. 158.**

The author hypothesizes that the cost of equity capital and the risk of U.S. multinational corporations will decrease relative to that of U.S. domestic companies. This is due to the maturing of attitudes on the parts of the host countries and the multinational companies themselves. Over the period 1965–78 host country – foreign business relations moved away from conflict toward cooperation. Catastrophic changes in national regimes for foreign investment have been replaced by a growing array of regulations to govern the activity of the foreign investor. Host countries (e.g. the Ancom countries) are more able and willing to state their requirements at the beginning of a venture, posing fewer changes during the life of the investment.

Ghadar, Fariborz, Stephen J. Kobrin, and Theodore H. Moran (eds.). *Managing International Political Risk: Strategies and Techniques.* **Washington, D.C: Ghadar Associates, 1983, p. 183.**

This edited collection is based on a conference held at Georgetown University under the auspices of the Overseas Private Investment Corporation. The book presents case studies on the management of political risk, analyses of the legal and financial aspects of risk management, an assessment of the costs and benefits of risk insurance, and an analysis of the role of political risk assessment in corporate strategic planning. Other topics include risk quantification, creeping expropriation, active vs. reactive postures toward risk and insurance for currency inconvertibility.

This book represents the second wave of academic and applied work on political risk: the management of risk. Although all the analytic concerns (quantitative vs. qualitative; macro vs. micro) have not been resolved, it is appropriate to evaluate the impact of such political analysis on the management and offsetting of political risk. The bottom line is the effectiveness of the firm in anticipating and responding to changes in its environment. That responsiveness is a function of analysis, management, decision and execution.

Gitman, Lawrence J., and John K. Forrester. "A Survey of Capital Budgeting Techniques Used by Major U.S. Firms." ***Financial Management.*** **6 (1977): 66-71.**

Gitman and Forrestor review the sophistication of capital budgeting procedures used in major U.S. corporations. Capital budgeting is one function that can and should be affected by political risk judgments. Conclusions are based on a written survey sent to 268 firms (110 replies) selected on the basis of their 1969 capital expenditures and their stock price growth between 1971 and 1976. Five varieties of capital budgeting were in use. The three most sophisticated were Net Present Value, Benefit/Cost Ratios, Internal Rate of Return. The less sophisticated methods were the Average Rate of Return and the Payback Period. Strong preferences were indicated by survey respondents for the more sophisticated methods.

The use of capital budgeting techniques occurs within a four stage process of project review. Project reviews begin with project definition and estimation of cash flows. The next stage is project analysis and selection. The third is project implementation. The last is project review. Capital budgeting has its greatest effect on the first stage. Political risk assessments can be incorporated into capital budgeting and project review. The survey indicated that three-fourths of the respondents were concerned about risk and uncertainty. In response to risk they would increase the project's minimum rate of return (44 percent), adjust the expected value of cash flows (27 percent), subjectively adjust expected value of cash flows (19 percent), and decrease the payback period (13 percent).

Gladwin, T.N., and I. Walter. "How Multinationals Can Manage Political and Social Forces." *Journal of Business Strategy.* **1(1), (Summer 1980): 54-68.**

Multinational corporations operating overseas face a wider variety of political and social risks than do those operating in the U.S.. Social and political conflict can have serious consequences for the operation of foreign subsidiaries. Corporations can adopt one or more responses to a conflict situation. These basic response types are compete, collaborate, compromise, avoid and accomodate. Each response is reviewed. Charts are included.

Gray, A. "Burr Hamilton Assesses Country Risk." *Banker's Magazine.* **164(1), (January/February 1981): 53-54.**

Investment banks are increasingly concerned with political risk overseas. Some banks are acquiring the physical and analytic capabilities seen in intelligence organizations. Burr Hamilton, for instance, has equipped itself with a crisis room occupied around the clock by senior officers of the bank. They are informed on a timely basis of political and economic developments around the world that may affect their investments and ability to move funds internationally. Burr Hamilton has established quick reaction mechanisms to move funds and investments in response to these changing environmental conditions.

Greene, Mark K. "The Management of Political Risk." *Bests Review: Property and Liability Insurance Edition.* **(July 1974): 71-74.**

Political risk is defined as the uncertainty derived from unanticipated acts of government or other organizations causing loss to business. Forms of risk include takeovers of equity, damage to plant and equipment, harm to personnel, restrictions on operations and financial activities, governmental interference, and discriminatory taxation. Sources of risk include opposition of local businesses to foreign competition, politics between governments and oppositions and problems in managing external economic balances. The political risk analyst can anticipate adverse changes by understanding key governmental actors, their behavior, values, and skills, and the stability of the regime itself. The corporation should also analyze its own products and operating style from the point of view of government regulators and local politicians. The assessment of the timing and probability of loss will shape the risk management strategy selected: avoidance, transfer, diversification, insurance or retention (riding it out).

Gunnemann, Jon P. (eds.). *The Nation-State and Transnational Corporations in Conflict: With Special Reference to Latin America.* **New York: Praeger Publishers, 1975, p. 242.**

This edited collection is based on a conference held at the Aspen Institute during September 1973 under the auspices of the Council on Religion and International Affairs. The general themes of the conference and the volume are the need for multinational companies in the developing countries, the legal and moral constraints that are, or should be, operating on the multinationals, the impact of regulation on economic performance and the behavior of the foreign investor, and the international flow of information about multinationals. Specific case studies include Dow's experience in Chile, IBM's operations in Latin America generally and the nationalization of Gulf Oil in Venezuela.

Gupta, Dipak K. "Multinational Investment in Yugoslavia: An Appraisal." *Columbia Journal of World Business.* **13(1), (Spring 1978): 71-79.**

Yugoslavia needs foreign investment to spur economic growth and innovation. But, Yugloslavs will be skeptical of foreign investors for several reasons. There is the customary tension between the needs of the global corporation and the host economy. There is the perception that the multinationals can manipulate price to their advantage and will maintain control over advanced technology. Economic planning and management can become hostage to the multinational. This last issue turns on the scale of investment and its sectoral concentration.

Potential investors face numerous obstacles in Yugoslavia. Only.joint ventures are permitted and only those with foreigners in a minority position. Foreign owners will face worker participation in the management of local enterprises. They may expect a low rate of return which will be denominated in dinars that are unconvertible internationally. Finally, potential investors lack understanding of the Yugoslav legal and political system and are likely to resolve such uncertainty through avoidance.

Haendel, Dan. *Foreign Investment: The Management of Political Risk.* **Boulder: Westview Press, 1978, p. 206.**

For Haendel "the political risk faced by foreign investors is defined as the risk or *probability* of occurrence of some political event(s) that will change the prospects for the profitability of a given investment." (p. 5). Effective management of political risk by the firm requires that risk be defined, identified continuously monitored, even after the investment has been made. Haendel reviews approaches to risk assessment including the dated (1960–66) Political System Stability Index (pp. 110–11) that is constructed from indicators of the socioeconomic condition of the country, indicators of the political and governmental processes, and measures of societal conflict. The resulting index is highly aggregated and has no tested or known relationship to political risk.

Haner, Frederick T. ***Global Business Strategy for the 1980s.*** **New York: Praeger Publishers, 1980; and "Business Environmental Risk Index."** ***Best's Review: Property Liability Insurance Edition.*** **(1975): 79–83**

Haner presents and evaluates techniques for forecasting conditions likely to affect international business. Economic, social, political and demographic variables are included. These measures of country potential are recommended for both long- and short-range operational planning and for new and existing investments. The Business Environmental Risk Index (BERI) is defined and its derivation is explained. This index measures for 45 countries worldwide the general quality of the business climate and the extent to which nationals are given preferential treatment over foreign businesses.

Herring, Richard (ed.). ***Managing International Risk: Essays Commissioned in Honor of the Centenary of the Wharton School.*** **New York: Cambridge University Press, 1983, p. 273.**

This edited collection is based on a conference sponsored by the Wharton School, University of Pennsylvania in October 1981. Papers focus on economic and political threats to the international economic system, social, cultural, economic and political aspects of country·risk, financial risk in lending to developing countries, organizational responses to country risk, specific practices of risk management underway at banks and manufacturing firms, and techniques for insuring against political risk.

Hershberger, Robert A., and John P. Noerager. "International Risk Management: Some Peculiar Considerations." ***Risk Management.*** **(April 1976): 23-34.**

Hershberger and Noerager argue that international risk management is analagous to domestic risk management but that the problems are more complex. International risk management requires all the same functions: (1) risk identification; (2) risk evaluation; (3) selection of risk management techniques; (4) risk management implementation; and, (5) control feedback. In addition to geographic and cultural distance, the international risk manager faces political and exchange or transfer risk (p. 23).

Specific factors relevant to the work of the international risk manager include geographic separation, organizational structure (centralization versus decentralization), differences in cultural outlook and managerial style, the economic development and current performance of the country, the host country legal environment, political risks arising from war, revolution, expropriation, contract/concession cancellation, exchange controls and discriminatory taxation or legislation.

To assess the likelihood of macro- level political risk the authors recommend looking at the country's history of self-government, the extent of unemployment in the economy, the equality of the income distribution, and the existence of constraints on social, economic, and political opportunity.

Howard, N. "Doing Business in Unstable Countries." *Dunn's Review.* **115(3), (March 1980): 48-55.**

Multinational companies have turned to consulting firms specializing in political risk assessment to predict future instability and devise corporate responses. Companies are beginning to realize the importance of political as well as economic analysis when making the decision to invest or make loans abroad. Extensive nationalization of U.S. assets, as well as recent turmoil in Iran, Central America and South Korea heighten awareness of political factors.

Hu, Hic. "Compensation in Expropriation: A Preliminary Economic Analysis." *Virginia Journal of International Law.* **20(1), (Fall 1979): 61-96.**

Expropriation is here to stay in the environment for international business. Compensation is a key aspect of relations between governments and companies. Hu argues that global economic efficiency should be the only end of compensation policy. The traditional standard of "prompt, adequate and effective" compensation is replaced by an estimation technique based on discounted cash flows, assuming no expropriation had taken place. Hu argues that compensation should be greater than fair market value in the case of investments that represent optimal inter- country capital flow (e.g. manufacturing investments in developing countries).

Jones, Randall J., Jr. "An Empirical Model of Political Risks in U.S. Oil Production Operations in Venezuela." *Paper Presented at the Annual Meeting of the International Studies Association.* **(Philadelphia, March 18-21, 1981): p. 28.**

This study focuses on the risks that have faced U.S. petroleum firms in Venezuela between 1952 and 1978. A model is developed to predict government actions against the industry up to and including nationalization. Discriminant analysis is used to classify the 11 years in which adverse government actions took place and the 16 years in which there were no acts against the industry. The model is based on relatively hard data from international organizations on GNP growth and industrial change. Government acts were coded from journalistic and trade sources. Political risk was found to be a function of declines in the rate of economic growth, declines in the rate of industrialization, and increases in the profitability of the oil industry, particularly after the 1973-74 oil shock.

Jones, Randall J., Jr. "A Model for Predicting Expropriation in Latin America, Applied to Jamaica." *Columbia Journal of World Business.* **15(1), (Spring 1980): 74-80.**

A model is derived from the expropriation experience of 21 Latin American countries during the period 1968-71 and applied to Jamaica. Variables included sociopolitical stability, government coercion of the opposition, the political strength of major opposition groups, the commitment of the government to economic modernization, and the government's foreign policy orientation. Several advanced statistical techniques (factor analysis, discriminant analysis, multiple regression) were used to construct indices from raw data and predict years in which expropriation is more likely. Three variables (riots, repression and UN voting patterns) were used to in the final model of expropriation propensity. The model was overdetermined. It overpredicted propensity to expropriate and indicated 1972 (the year of Manley's election) as the most risky, rather than 1974 when expropriation actually took place. The author argues that 1972 set the stage for the subsequent nationalization and that the model provides a leading indicator of political risk.

Juhl, Paulgeorg. "Investment Climate Indicators: Are They Useful Devices to Foreign Investors?" *Management International Review.* **2 (1978): 45-50.**

Juhl reviews the political risk service provided by the Business Environmental Risk Index. BERI focuses on discriminatory treatment of foreigners and the overall climate for business. These are two very general concepts. BERI has provided quarterly forecasts for 45 countries since 1972. The Index is based on information about politics, business operations, finance and nationalism. An empirical analysis between BERI's measure of nationalism and investment flows is presented. The results are inconclusive. What should be analyzed is the relationship between BERI's indicators and subsequent policy actions of the host government. These actions, in turn, will effect the investment behavior of foreign business.

Kamanu, Onyeonoro S. "Compensation for Expropriation in the Third World." *Studies in Comparative International Development.* **10 (Summer 1975): 3-21.**

Kamanu examines the circumstances in which the application of the traditional legal standard for payment of compensation for nationalized investments ("prompt, adequate and effective") would be unfair or unreasonable. He argues for a fair compensation based on the interests of both parties. Factors to examine before compensation could be determined include the relative shares of input factors (foreign capital and local labor), secondary benefits and costs to the host country of foreign investment, and, practices of transfer pricing on the part of the multinational firm.

Kassicieh, W. K., and J. R. Nassar. "Political Risk and the Multinational Corporation: A Study of the Impact of the Iranian Revolution on Saudi Arabia, Kuwait, and the United Arab Emirates." *Management International Review.* **22(3), (July 1982): 22-32.**

This study examines the possible spillover effects of the Iranian revolution and the continuing Iran-Iraq war on stability in the Persian Gulf. Certain characteristics of pre-revolutionary Iran are shared by the Gulf states: an explosion of the gross national product and a great need for infrastructure development in the face of rapid social mobilization. Given these similarities, the authors test whether multinationals have slowed the pace of investment in the Gulf. Testing average levels before and after the revolution in Iran, the authors find no difference in level of sales or contracts in the Gulf states. The number of new subsidiaries did decline, however, indicating some concern about the future stability (economic or political) of the Gulf.

Keegan, Warren S. "Multinational Scanning: A Study of the Information Sources Utilized by HQs Executives in Multinational Companies." *Administrative Science Quarterly.* **19 (1974): 411-21.**

Keegan drew a sample of multinational corporations based in the United States and interviewed executives with responsibilities for international operations. Executives were selected if they had received and passed on information about the external environment's impact on the firm. These interviews indicated the importance of human sources of information and sources outside the United States. These last were primarily local company managers. Service organizations (money center banks) were the next most important source of information on country risk. Documents were the next most important source. Here the key publications were the *Wall Street Journal* and the *New York Times.* There was little reliance on systematic scanning methods or computer-based information systems. Even manual "shoeboxes" for storing data were seldom used. There were also substantial intracorporate barriers to information flow that weakened political risk assessment.

Kelly, Marie Wicks. *Foreign Investment Evaluation Practices of U.S. Multinational Corporations.* **Ann Arbor: UMI Research Press, 1980, p. 232.**

This empirical study focuses on the foreign investment evaluation practices of U.S. based industrial corporations. A structured questionnaire was mailed to 255 companies that were multinational (at least one international direct investment), large (on the 1977 *Fortune 500* list) and in manufacturing.

The mail questionnaire was directed to the chief financial officer or treasurer to obtain information about the corporation's most recent investment. Information was collected on the following variables: geographic area, time period, size, ownership structure, and method of investment. This information was used to analyze relationships between investment activity, parent firm characteristics, and risk evaluation practices of these major international firms.

Kobrin, Stephen J. *Managing Political Risk Assessment: Strategic Response to Environmental Challenge.* **Los Angeles: University of California Press, 1982, p. 224.**

The interaction of organizations and environments is the dominant theme of this empirical analysis of political risk assessment. As American companies have become more active in trade and investment overseas since World War II, the impact of political factors on the performance of the firm has increased substantially. Corporate efforts to understand political change in unfamiliar environments and their potential impact on operations have also increased, particularly during the 1970s.

Assessment practices of U.S.-based, international firms were ascertained through quantitative questionnaires, supplemented by in-depth personal interviews. Questionnaires were received from 455 firms selected for the mail questionnaire from a population of all U.S. industrial firms that had more than $100 million in sales in 1976 and that had a minimum of one foreign subsidiary. The survey was conducted between August and November 1978 to evaluate political risk assessment practices underway at that time and the extent of management's satisfaction with those practices. A response rate of 42 percent provided a generous empirical foundation on which to base conclusions about the factors that affect the structure, function, and success of political assessment in large, industrial firms.

Responses to this unique Conference Board survey were analyzed quantitatively using contingency tables and logit analysis to explain inter- corporate differences in the organization and function of political assessment. The institutionalization of political assessment was a function of firm size (global sales), the percentage of total sales generated abroad, the number of countries in which the firm is operating and the organizational structure of the firm. Other major topics treated include the organization of the assessment function, managerial perceptions of political risk, techniques for scanning foreign political environments, and the practical use of political judgments.

Kobrin, Stephen J. "Political Assessment by International Firms: Models or Methodologies?" *Journal of Policy Modelling.* **3(2), (May 1981): 251-270.**

Kobrin examines the impact of politics on multinational industrial firms and how these corporations have responded analytically and managerially to the explosion of political risk throughout the Third World during the 1970s. Political risk is accepted as an unavoidable aspect of international business and techniques for making complex political judgments are presented and compared. Corporate practices are reviewed on the basis of interviews with risk practitioners and a detailed written questionnaire mailed to major U.S.-based companies with substantial international activities.

Kobrin, Stephen J. "Political Risk: A Review and Reconsideration." *Journal of International Business Studies.* **1 (Spring/Summer 1979): 67-80.**

Kobrin reviews the literature dealing with the assessment and management of political risk by multinational enterprises. This article builds on previous work by more precisely defining political risk and suggesting means for integrating political risk assessment into the decision-making process. Areas for further research are suggested.

Kraar, L. "The Multinationals Get Smarter About Political Risks." *Fortune.* **101(6), (March 24, 1980): 86-100.**

The Iranian Revolution stimulated American corporations considering investments overseas to scrutinize the political, economic and social conditions in order to assess the level of risk. While Iran is not the only country in which American companies have suffered losses to political risk, the loss there was so extensive that it has given rise to a whole new industry. Losses in Iran were comparable to those in Cuba almost twenty years before. But the supply of analysts and techniques and the general perception of the part of corporate managers that political risk is here to stay account for the emergence of this new industry: international political and social analysis.

Kuhn, W. E. "The Hickenlooper Amendment as a Determinant of the Outcome of Expropriation Disputes." ***Social Science Journal.*** **14 (January 1971): 71-81.**

Kuhn reviews the application and non- application of the Hickenlooper Amendment to the U.S. Foreign Assistance Act of 1962 to expropriations in Ceylon (1962), Brazil (1962), Indonesia (1965), Chile under Presidents Frei and Allende, Peru (1968) and Bolivia (1969). Kuhn demonstrates how the Hickenlooper Amendment fell short of its goals. It did not enhance respect in the Third World for private business property and it soured relations between the U.S. Government and many developing countries. Despite its mandatory provisions, the executive branch consistently was able to avoid applying Hickenlooper. An explanation of this is offered by Einhorn (1974) in an analysis of the IPC case.

LaPalombara, Joseph. "Assessing the Political Environment for Business: A New Role for Political Scientists." ***PS*** **15(2), (Spring 1982): 180-86.**

LaPalombara reviews the factors that have increased the salience of the political environment for corporate managers. These are (1) the post-colonial explosion of nation-states; (2) changing patterns of international trade and investment; (3) burgeoning public sectors in much of the developing world; (4) increasing sophistication of regulations and regulators; (5) declining profit margins; (6) competitive pressures; (7) political upheavals in developing countries and political change in developed market economies (e.g. France under Mitterand and the U.K under Thatcher); and, (8) the increasing sophistication of international managers.

Political analysts must respond to the practical needs of these corporate managers. Their concern is to reduce uncertainty in the planning process. They operate with short-term horizons and are invariably short of time. Hence, they will have little patience for political analysis that is academic in substance or tone. However, "(c)onsumers of political risk analysis want assessments to be more rigorous, systematic and, above all, more sophisticated then in the past." (p. 181). This concern for an improved product provides the opportunity for academics provided they can adapt to the requirements and mores of private industry.

Lax, D.A., and J.K. Sebenius. "Insecure Contracts and Resource Development." *Public Policy.* **29(4), (Fall 1981): 418-436.**

Third World mineral development has declined in recent years. Rising concern about expropriation is responsible along with forced contract renegotiation. The authors present an analysis of investor-host country contracts. Performance bonds, political risk insurance, linkage and prevention as means of risk offsetting are discussed. Principles and mechanisms to resolve instabilities are discussed.

Lax, Howard L. ***Political Risk in the International Oil and Gas Industry.*** **Boston: International Human Resources Development Corp., 1983, p. 195.**

Lax begins by defining political risk, distinguishing its various types, and explaining why political risk assessment is an increasing corporate function. Political risk management is an essential aspect of decision-making in large international companies. The international petroleum industry is analyzed in the following terms: politicization of oil (resource nationalism, evolution of concession agreements, OPEC, conflicting goals of the oil company and its host government), the substance and structure of the international oil and gas industry, risks and resources (expropriation, development, production), and the nature of political risk.

Major approaches to risk assessment are reviewed. These include BERI, BI, WPRF, Shell's ASPRO/SPAIR, and the Political System Stability Index (PSSI). Key risk events that analysts should be anticipating are, according to Lax, foreign war, civil disorder, total expropriation, "creeping" expropriation, costly fiscal changes (taxes, royalties), price increases, domestic price controls, production controls, export/sales restrictions, remittance restrictions, exchange controls, devaluation or revaluation, embargoes or boycotts, re-investment requirements, domestic refining/shipping demands, direct government-to- government sales policies, ancilliary demands (hiring, promotion, training of nationals), and ideological changes.

Libby, Ronald T., and James H. Cobbe. "Regime Change in Third World Extractive Industries: A Critique." ***International Organization.*** **35(4), (Autumn 1981): 725-44.**

Libby and Cobbe critique an earlier study (Jodice, 1980) on the propensity of Third World governments to expropriate foreign investment in the resource sector (petroleum extraction and mining and smelting). This critique reviews problems of data collection and measurement, data analysis and conceptual approaches to political risk assessment.

Lillich, Richard B. "Requiem for Hickenlooper." *American Journal of International Law.* **69 (January 1975).**

Lillich discusses the effects of the Foreign Assistance Act of 1973 on the Hickenlooper Amendment. Hickenlooper was originally a response to the Cuban nationalizations of U.S. property. A frustrated Congress mandated termination of U.S. foreign aid to any country that nationalized U.S. investments without "prompt, adequate and effective compensation." The 1973 act effectively gutted Hickenlooper by deleting the clause requiring mandatory application. In fact, Hickenlooper had been applied only once, to Ceylon, and was generally seen in Washington as counter-productive to the full range of American foreign policy objectives.

Lillich, Richard B. "The United States-Hungarian Claims Agreement of 1973." *American Journal of International Law.* **69 (July 1975): 534-59.**

After twenty-five years of on and off negotiation, the U.S.-Hungarian settlement was signed on March 6, 1973. The agreement provided for a lump sum payment of almost 20 million dollars to the U.S. Government and private citizens as compensation for losses due to war, nationalizations and financial debts. This settlement represented one-fourth of total claims and was to be dispensed in twenty annual claims. Lillich reviews the eligibility provisions of the agreement and evaluates it in terms of international claims practice.

Lillich, Richard B. *The Valuation of Nationalized Property in International Law.* **Charlottesville: University of Virginia Press, 1972.**

Substantial nationalizations (Cuba, Chile, Peru) increased the significance of the valuation problem. Lillich identifies and recommends solutions to problems of valuing nationalized property. Essays are organized into four categories. The first set develops principles for compensation based on the value of the firm to the host country after nationalization. The second group looks at current international practice (Spain, Great Britain, Austria). A third section examines U.S. policy with special reference to the Cuban nationalizations and the activities of the Foreign Claims Settlement Commission. A fourth group of essays proposes the transmutation of municipal law standards (based on U.S., Canadian, and British law) into an international standard.

Lipson, Charles. "The Development of Expropriation Insurance: The Role of Corporate Preferences and State Initiatives." *International Organization.* **32(2), (Spring 1978): 351-76.**

Lipson documents the development of U.S. investment insurance programs from the early years of the Marshall Plan to 1974. Original insurance for currency inconvertibility expanded to include risks of expropriation and damage from civil war and insurrection. Two factors,operating in harmony, promoted the growth of U.S. insurance programs: corporate preferences and initiatives by policymakers.

Lloyd, Bruce. "The Identification and Assessment of Political Risk in the International Environment." *Long Range Planning.* **(December 1974): pp. 24-32.**

Lloyd asks where politics fit into the risk return judgment in investment decisionmaking. He begins by examining the reasons why companies expose themselves to political risks. A second section focuses on sources of international political risk. The paper concludes with an evaluation of alternative risk management techniques.

Lloyd, Bruce. *Political Risk Management.* **London: Keith Shipton Developments, Ltd., 1976, p. 60.**

Lloyd's brief monograph covers most of the major issues involved in political risk identification, evaluation, and management. Political risk and risk management are defined, the corporation's role in society is evaluated, the relevance to risk of the corporation's own objectives is assessed. The economic role of government and its impact on international business is also reviewed. The question of social and political stability is directly addressed. Foreign exchange risk and integrating these judgments into the investment decision process are presented. Lloyd concludes with recommendations for applying risk management techniques. He stays clear of debates over the role of the state in the economy or the net effect of foreign direct investment on capital-importing countries.

Factors leading to instability are discussed. These include strong internal factions, social unrest and disorder, recent or impending independence, forthcoming elections, and proximity to armed conflict. Alternative measures of political instability developed by leading scholars are presented.

Factors limiting the effectiveness of political risk management are also discussed. The major limitation on effective risk management has been, according to Lloyd, the widespread belief among businessmen that they have an "inalienable right" to conduct their business and that all external criticism is by definition, unreasonable. Businessmen have traditionally not appreciated the varying views of local pressure groups.

To counteract these tendencies, Lloyd recommends a project-specific approach to political risk that objectively analyzes the likely results of the project (including effects on the host country), the identification of all local groups that may have an interest in the proposed project, the evaluation of likely responses by these political actors to the proposed investment, the comparison of the objectives of the project with the arms of local and national government, and, the establishment of a corporate information strategy to assess changes in the operating environment before and after the investment has taken place. Specific risk management strategies are also discussed: avoidance, risk transfer, risk retention, and risk reduction.

Lowenfeld, Andreas F. "Act of State and Department of State: First National City Bank v. *Banco Nacional De Cuba.*" *American Journal of International Law.* 66 (October 1972): 795-814.

Lowenfeld examines the role of domestic courts in the ajudication of disputes arising from the sovereign acts of another nation. In the case of *Banco Nacional de Cuba v. Sabbatino* the issue of setting judicial limits in U.S. constitutional practice was raised.

MacKenzie, I. "Political Risk Insurance Examined." *National Underwriter - Property and Casualty Insurance.* 86(42), (October 15, 1982): 2-47.

The market for private political risk insurance has grown at a substantial rate over the past few years. Private underwriters are filling gaps in the coverage offered by public insurance agencies. Private companies are selling coverage at rates that are less favorable than those offered by public agencies - especially the quasi-public Overseas Private Investment Corporation. Private insurers also have less influence on foreign governments than do public insurance agencies. For these reasons, argues MacKenzie, capacity to underwrite political risk by private insurers is declining. The author recommends an international agency to insure against political risk.

Micallef, Joseph. "Political Risk Assessment." *Columbia Journal of World Business.* **16(2), (Summer 1981): 47-52.**

Micallef details the elements of an effective political risk assessment system. First, the analyst identifies factors that pose risks to foreign investment. Second, he develops a time-sensitive monitoring system based on those factors. Third, changes in the risk profile of a country or specific project are incorporated into the corporation's long-term planning. Fourth, protective strategies are devised, particularly against the threat of expropriation.

Montgomery, David B., and Charles B. Weinberg. "Toward Strategic Intelligence Systems." *Journal of Marketing.* **1979 (43): 41-52.**

Examples of strategic intelligence systems (SIS) include BCG's growth/share matrix, ADL's life cycle strategy, Shell's directional policy matrix, and GE's stoplight strategy matrix. An SIS provides three forms of intelligence. Defensive intelligence alerts the organization to changes in the environment that challenge operating assumptions. Passive intelligence provides benchmark data for objective evaluations. Offensive intelligence identifies opportunities. Based on interviews with 100 executives in 30 companies, Montgomery and Weinberg describe the elements of a SIS (competition, technology, customers, political risks, and social change), functions (priorities, indicators, collection, and analyses) and sources of intelligence (government under the Freedom of Information Act, competitors, suppliers, customers, profesisonal meetings and the media). Any SIS is only as good as the information on which its judgments are based.

Moran, Theodore H. "Transnational Strategies of Protection and Defense by Multinational Corporations: Spreading the Risk and Raising the Cost for Nationalization in Natural Resources." *International Organization.* **27(2), (Spring 1973): 273-87.**

This study focuses on the copper industry in Chile from the end of World War II to the final nationalizations of the investments of Kennecott and Anaconda by Allende during 1971. The study details Kennecott's strategy of investment protection which was developed during the late 1960s. This was a response to corporate decisions to increase investments in the face of increasing risk of nationalization. A private strategy of developing international financial and contractual linkages to circumscribe the flexibility of the Chilean government was implemented because of a lack of confidence in the ability or willingness of the U.S. Government to defend U.S.-based multinationals. Anaconda's inaction in this regard contrasts unfavorably with Kennecott's proactive stance toward political risk.

Moran, Theodore H. (ed.). *International Political Risk Assessment: The State of the Art.* **Washington, D.C: Georgetown University, 1980, p. 79.**

This conference-based volume provides an overview of political risk assessment techniques as practiced by specific U.S. companies. An overview of the field is provided by Moran. He details sources of corporate bargaining strength and presents strategies to offset vulnerability. Factors affecting bargaining power include the size of the fixed investment, the importance of initial vs. incremental investments, the stability or maturity of the technology, the level of concentration of the industry, the existence of monopolistic or oligopolistic power downstream, and, for manufacturing investments, the importance of product differentiation or brand name loyalty. Stephen Kobrin emphasizes the selectivity of risk and argues for analytic approaches that are objective, systematic, convergent and functionally related to the investment decision process. Contributors describe political risk assessment at the Bank of America, Exxon and Risk Insights, Inc.

Much, M. "GM's Watchdog for Foreign Political Risk." *Industry Week.* **204(7), (March 31, 1980): 79-82.**

Political analysis is a relatively new aspect of American corporate life. While government relations has always been important to the domestic operations of major U.S. corporations, foreign political risk analysis is a recent phenomenon. General Motors hired Gordon Rayfield as their senior political risk analyst for countries where GM has large direct investments.

Nagy, P. J. *Country Risk: How to Assess, Quantify, and Monitor It.* **London: Euromoney Publications, 1979; and, "Quantifying Country Risk: A System Developed by Economists at the Bank of Montreal."** *Columbia Journal of World Business.* **(Fall 1978): pp. 135-147.**

Written from the perspective of international banking, these studies provide useful introductions to the concept of risk. Country risk, sovereign risk, and political risk are defined. Approaches to risk assessment are discussed. A series of checklists and structured questionnaires are presented that can be used to evaluate investment climate overseas.

Nehemkis, Peter. "Expropriation has a Silver Lining." *California Management Review.* **17 (Fall 1974): 15-22.**

Nehemkis establishes the importance of expropriation as a form of political risk. In 1970-74, 34 LDCs expropriated approximately $1.2 billion of U.S. foreign investment. Much of this was, of course, concentrated in Chile. In 1973 U.S. companies purchased $2.3 billion in investment insurance from OPIC. These extensive risks call for skilfull management and alertness to opportunities for negotiation and compromise. Any negotiator for the multinational enterprise should keep the following factors in mind. What is the state of U.S. relations with the host country? What role might other U.S. investors in the host country play (hostages?)? How credible is my firm as a good corporate citizen? Nehemkis uses the experience of ITT in Chile as an example of how not to manage political risk.

Nehrt, Lee Charles. "The Political Climate for Foreign Investment." *Business Horizons.* **15 (June 1972): 51-8; and,** *The Political Environment for Foreign Investment: With Special Reference to North Africa.* **New York: Praeger, 1970, p. 391**

Nehrt presents a model of the political climate based on statements and actions of political leaders, the actions of the government, and the historical policy of the country toward foreign business. Government actions to encourage and discourage business are examined. Other relevant variables include the country's history, colonization, social development and foreign relations. Case studies are developed for Algeria, Morocco and Tunisia.

O'Leary, Michael K., and William D. Coplin. ***Quantitative Techniques and Foreign Policy Analysis and Forecasting.*** **New York: Praeger Publishers, 1975, p. 291.**

Under the auspices of E. Raymond Platig of the State Department's Bureau of Intelligence and Research, Coplin and O'Leary present commissioned research that attempts to bridge the gap between in-house analysis and academic approaches to foreign policy. Government political analysts are skeptical about quantitative techniques for three reasons. These are: (1) quantitative methods are too complex, (2) these methods are inconclusive, and, (3) they are far removed from the practical concerns of policymakers and analysts.

This study begins with a brief overview of the use of social science techniques at the State Department. A second section contains six case studies, applying different quantitative techniques to a wide range of analytic problems. These case studies are:

(1) Predicting political instability in Black Africa,

(2) Elections forecasting in France, Italy, and Finland,

(3) Explaining cross-national differences in military spending throughout Latin America,

(4) ·Export-generated data on North-South Korean bargaining,

(5) Forecasting violence in the Middle East, and,

(6) Modelling international coalitions in global oil politics.

O'Leary, Michael K., and William D. Coplin. *Political Risk in Thirty Countries.* **London: Euromoney Publications, 1981, p. 210.**

This publication documents the coverage and procedures used in the preparation of Frost and Sullivan's *World Political Risk Forecasts.* Countries reviewed are: Argentina, Bolivia, Brazil, Canada, Chile, China, Colombia, Greece, India, Indonesia, Iran, Israel, Italy, Mexico, Nigeria, Pakistan, Peru, Philippines, Portugal, Saudi Arabia, Singapore, South Africa, Spain, Taiwan, Thailand, Turkey, Venezuela, Yugoslavia, Zaire and Zambia. Technical appendices include data from country specialists, country questionnaires and the use of models for aggregating results. Cross-national analysis compared underlying sources of risk, critical political developments, potential for political instability and government restrictions.

The analytic model is based on issues, politically active groups, the issue position of those groups, the salience of the issues to those groups and the power that they can bring to bear on the government to attain their objectives. Factors underlying political risk include country economic performance, country vulnerability to changes in the international markets for its products, the demands of external financial institutions, international political conflict and domestic instability.

Olson, Richard S. "Environmental Risk Assessment: Suggested Directions." *Paper Presented at the Annual Meeting of the International Studies Association.* **(Philadelphia: March 18-20, 1981): p. 24.**

Olson examines political risk assessment as a species of applied research. Environmental risk assessment includes political, social, economic and natural factors that affect corporate performance. Applied research, often disparaged by scholars, can make a lasting contribution if it has a strong theoretical base. The utility of applied research and its staying power will be enhanced by its ability to make predictive statements.

Overholt, William H. "Forecasting Political Stability and Instability." *Paper Presented at the Hudson Institute Conference on Political-Economic Forecasting for Policymakers.* **Croton-on-Hudson, New York: June 22-23, 1979.**

Overholts presents an analytic framework for understanding political change. The key variables are political organizations. Regime organizations are conflicting with dissident organizations. Drawing insights from psychological conditions or economic trends is useful but will remain incomplete without an explicit analysis of the group context of political action. Overholt emphasizes the social basis of the regime, governmental institutions and the character of the leadership.

Pechota, V. "The 1981 United States-Czechoslovak Claims Settlement Agreement - An Epilogue to Post-War Nationalization and Expropriation Disputes." *American Journal of International Law.* **76(3), (July 1982): 639-53.**

After 35 years of negotiations the United States and Czechoslovakia reached an agreement to settle claims arising out of the nationalizations of 1945 (mines, banks and insurance) and the socialization of the entire economy in 1948. This agreement was the last to be reached with the

East European states and was unprecendented in the willingness of the Czechs to pay compensation equal to 100 percent of the principle taken.

Piper, Don C. "Protecting American Property Abroad: Customary International Law and Bilateral Treaties." *Paper Presented at the Annual Meeting of the International Studies Association.* **(Washington, D.C., 1977): p. 51.**

Piper reviews the development of international law governing expropriation from the 1930s, patterns of expropriation, U.S. policy, and codes of conduct emanating from the U.N. General Assembly and the OECD. The core of international law in this area is the bilateral treaty of "Friendship, Commerce and Navigation." These agreements serve as the basis for U.S investment guaranties and insurance plans. The paper also reviews the applicability of traditional standards of compensation (prompt, adequate and effective) in the light of twentieth-century practice and the inherent ambiguity of those standards.

Preble, John F. "Corporate Use of Environmental Scanning." *University of Michigan Business Review.* **30 (1978): 12-17.**

The external environment consists of the marketplace, technological innovation, external growth, government policy and the larger political-social environment. The corporate scanner should seek information about events and their interrelationships outside the corporation to aid management. Environmental scanning can help a corporation organize, design and develop its internal structure by illuminating problem areas; agenda setting for top management; educating management and informing product decisions. Preble discusses ten predictive techniques that are relevant to these tasks: extrapolation, historical analogy, intuitive reasoning, scenario building, cross-impact matrices, morphological analysis, network methods, model building, Delphi techniques and a missing link approach.

Radcliffe, J. "The Way to Cope with Political Risk." *Euromoney.* **(May 1980): 147-8.**

Beginning with the Iranian revolution there has been a massive increase in the political risk insurance business for both investors and contractors. But, bank guarantees have often not been effective protection for contractors exposed to unpredictable calling risks. Conditional surety bonds are a more promising insurance device for contractors who must operate overseas under volatile political conditions.

Radetzki, Marian. "Has Political Risk Scared Mineral Investment Away From the Deposits in Developing Countries?" *World Development.* **10 (January 1982): 39-48.**

Widespread nationalizations and selective expropriations have combined to alter irrevocably the structure of foreign direct investment in mineral extraction in the Third World. Radetzki reviews the literature and data on mineral investment flows. He argues that both flow and stock data understate the activity of mineral corporations in the Third World.

Ralston, A. "Before Investing Overseas." *Security Management.* **26(2), (February 1982): 46-51.**

The value or operations of any business firm can be affected by political risk. Political risk covers many forms of governmental behavior including seizure of assets, contract cancellation and regulations governing international capital flows. Firms planning an investment in a foreign country are spending more of their time and resources anticipating political changes and developing corporate responses. Political risk analysis is most effective when it is country or project specific. Access to information in the host country is a key factor in the shaping of a political risk assessment. Once analyzed, the firm can manage political risk through avoidance, structuring of investment finance, and contract design.

Ralston, A. "The Struggle to Protect Worldwide Investment." *Risk Management. 28(4), (April 1981): 70-4.*

Political risk insurance is offered by public agencies of all OECD states. In the U.S., public insurance is offered by the Federal Credit Insurance Association in cooperation with the Export- Import Bank. The Overseas Private Investment Corporation (OPIC) was created in 1971 to consolidate various federal insurance programs. OPIC is a federally chartered insurance agency. Its Congressional mandate requires that it be managed in a business-like manner and operate on the basis of its income from insurance premiums. OPIC insurance is available for new investments in developing countries if the investment has the approval of the host government, can be shown to benefit the socioeconomic development of that country, and is not injurious to U.S. employment or balance of payments goals.

Robinson, John. *Multinationals and Political Control.* **New York: St. Martin's Press, 1983, p. 507.**

Robinson reviews supranational codes of conduct for multinational companies developed by the OECD, the UN and the EC and examines the outlook for international regulation of the multinational corporation during the 1980s. Unlike the resolutions of the UN or the OECD, EC policy has the force of law and is binding on multinationals operating in the ten member states. Robinson examines the operation of OECD guidelines in Belgium, Spain, Denmark, Sweden, the U.K., Finland and the Netherlands in such areas as unionization, worker participation in management, employment protection, production transfers and plant closures. Substantial appendices are included reporting the text of these codes of conduct, data on investment flows and the number and turnover of multinationals by country of origin.

Robinson, Richard D. ***National Control of Foreign Business Entry: A Survey of Fifteen Countries.*** **New York: Praeger Publishers, 1976, p. 508.**

Robinson reviews the investment entry controls of fifteen developing and developed countries: Burma, Indonesia, Malaysia, Thailand, the Philippines, Bolivia, Brazil, Chile, Colombia, Ecuador, Mexico, Peru, Venezuela, Japan and Sweden. Robinson discusses investment flows, the entry process, entry criteria, and evaluates the overall effects of host country entry requirements. Common entry conditions are agreements to meet specific targets in the areas of growth rates, development of local expertise, local employment, the transfer of management control to locals and the eventual indigenization of ownership.

Rogers, Jerry (ed.). ***Global Risk Assessments: Issues, Concepts and Applications.*** **Riverside, CA: Global Risk Assessments, Inc: 1983, p. 175.**

The theme of this collection of original articles is that political risk analysts should perform with high analytic standards but remember that they are operating in a corporate and political world. Rogers brings together scholars and practitioners to present views on how political risk can be analyzed and how these analytic products can best be incorporated into the decision-making process. Twelve articles deal with the assessment of the environment for international business, country and trade risk assessment, and the management of political risk. Sassi and Dil present their experience at Gulf's International Policy Analysis unit. Doyle presents a systems framework under consideration at Canada's Export Development Corporation that would replace the current bifurcation of political and economic analysis. Richard Li presents a complex technical analysis of methods for integrating political risk judgments into the capital budgeting process. Contributors emphasize the need for political risk analysts to fit well into the corporate structure and adjust their methods to those that are acceptable to management. "People skills may be as important for a political analyst in the corporate environment as his analytic abilities." (p. 24).

Rosenn, Keith S. "Expropriation in Argentina and Brazil: Theory and Practice." ***Virginia Journal of International Law.*** **15(2), (Winter 1975): 277-318.**

Expropriation is a legal device for affecting social and economic change. Causes of expropriation are reviewed. Traditional standards of international law and due process are upheld in theory in Argentina and Brazil. Actual practice is another matter. Rosenn writes of the "grand larceny of inflation" and the "petit larceny of policy and tax powers". Restrictions on profit repatriation, capital repatriation and borrowing were applied against foreigners in a discriminatory manner. This was particularly pointed during the Vargas and Peron dictatorships. Rosenn reviews concession agreements in Argentina and Brazil governing extractive industries.

Rubin, Seymour J. "Developments in the Law and Institutions of International Economic Relations: The Multinational Enterprise at Bay." *American Journal of International Law.* **68(3), (July 1974): 475-88.**

Contrary to the conventional wisdom of the early 1970s, Rubin argues that the multinational enterprise (MNE) is at bay, rather than the nation- state. The MNE is a large bureaucratic structure. As such it lacks flexibility and will not demonstrate the initiative often associated with private sector organizations (at least in the mind of public-sector critics). The mobility of the MNE is also overstated. Firms acquire a stake in the host country derived from trained employees, precious ores, and investments in plant and equipment. Multinationals may have manipulated governments. They have also been tools of foreign or domestic policy, particularly those of the U.S. Government. Examples of the latter include U.S. restrictions on international capital movements and trading strategic goods and minerals with communist countries. The international ambience of the MNE has changed drastically. Host country, home state and international codes of conduct reduce the autonomy and scope of operations of the MNE.

Rubin Seymour J. "Developments in the Law and Institutions of International Economic Relations: Reflections Concerning the United Nations Commission on Transnational Corporations." *American Journal of International Law.* **70(1), (January 1976): 73-91.**

Rubin discusses the formation of the U.N. Commission, the character of the Group of Eminent Persons and the mandate and resources of the Centre on Transnational Corporations. The main function of the Centre is to increase the information about transnational companies available to Third World countries. Efforts to formulate a code of conduct for private companies are also reviewed.

Rummel, Rudolph J., and David A. Heenan. "How Multinationals Analyze Political Risk." ***Harvard Business Review.*** **56(1), (January-February, 1978): 67-76.**

Rummel and Heenan review four basic approaches to political risk assessment used by major American industrial corporations and financial institutions. The "Grand Tours" by senior corporate executives are widespread but produce "an overdose of selective information" according to the authors. The "Old Hands" method draws on the expertise of diplomats, journalists and businessmen in shaping a picture of the political future of a given country. More systematically, the Delphi technique identifies variables, asks experts to make judgments about those variables, and aggregates those judgments into a final projection. Quantitative techniques, including multivariate analysis, are used by a small number of firms and consulting organizations to isolate and monitor factors effecting the environment for international business.

Using Indonesia as a test case, Rummel and Heenan propose a methodology (factor analysis) that will use quantitative measures of national political and economic performance to produce a ranking of countries in terms of political risk. When integrated with the other techniques, the authors expect this formal and quantitative methodology to increase the precision and prescience of political risk analysis.

Sacks, Paul M., and Stephen Blank. "Forecasting Political Risk." *Corporate Director.* **2(11), (September/October 1981): 9-14.**

Based on surveys conducted by the Conference Board, Sacks and Blank conclude that most executives use some sort of international risk analysis before approving a major investment or project in a foreign country. However, there is not any proven methodology or widely accepted approach for political risk forecasting. Five principles of country risk assessment are developed. A guide to new forecasting services is provided.

Seidl-Hohenveldern, Ignaz. "Austrian Practice of Lump-Sum Compensation by Treaty." *American Journal of International Law.* **70(4), (October 1976): 763-77.**

Austrian practices of negotiating compensation agreements and methods for dispensing of lump-sum agreements are reviewed. With the notable exception of the United States, such practices are poorly documented. Seidl-Hohenveldern's work partially remedies that gap in the international legal literature. The role of the judiciary is examined in the light of the ability of the Austrian state to select which claims it chooses to pursue.

Seidl-Hohenveldern, Ignaz. "Chilean Copper Nationalization Cases Before German Courts." *American Journal of International Law.* **69(1), (January 1975): 110-19.**

West German courts did not recognize the legality of Chilean nationalizations of copper company assets because the takings were discriminatory, appropriate compensation was lacking, and there was a denial of justice. Nonetheless, the Hamburg Superior Court denied the motion to attach a shipment of copper from Chile that had been exported to Hamburg. Seidl- Hohenveldern reviews the Court's reasoning and assesses the implications of the decision.

Shapiro, Alan C. "Managing Political Risk: A Policy Approach." *Columbia Journal of World Business.* **16(3), (Fall 1981): 63-69.**

Shapiro argues for a more formal assessment process that is firm or project specifc and tied into the investment and risk management planning. Corporate planners need to develop a three step approach to political risk. First, they need to identify the sources of risk, forecast its likelihood, and assess its probable consequences. Second, they need to develop policies in advance to cope with risk (avoidance, insurance, negotiation, investment structuring). Third, in the event that expropriation occurs, they need to develop measures to maximize compensation.

Simon, Jeffrey D. "Political Risk Assessment: Past Trends and Future Prospects." *Columbia Journal of World Business.* **17 (Fall 1982): 62-71.**

Simon provides an excellent review of a decade of scholarly research on political risk (ten authors are reviewed) as well as the application of risk assessment techniques in eight different corporations and consulting firms. For each of these eighteen approaches, Simon presents their definition of risk, the type of analysis undertaken, database used if any, and key variables incorporated in the analysis. The author continues by developing a general framework for identifying risk and provides guidelines for multinational companies interested in developing their own in-house risk monitoring capability.

Simon's general framework clusters variables according to their level of measurement (macro v. micro); their functional significance (government v. social groups); and their international status (internal v. external). This Early Warning System will enable the corporate political analyst to monitor changes in existing conditions, reduce surprise and provide increased lead time to adapt corporate policy to new conditions.

Smith, David N., and Louis T. Wells, Jr. "Mineral Agreements in Developing Countries: Structures and Substance." *American Journal of International Law.* **69 (July 1975): 560-90.**

The production contract is currently the modal arrangement between governments and mining companies, replacing the traditional concession agreement dominant until the late 1960s. Changes in government - industry relations have been influenced by relative bargaining strengths, structure of the industry concerned, host country concern with sovereignty and local control, and the information level and negotiating skills of each party. Smith and Wells distinguish three types of agreements: the traditional concession, the modern concession and production sharing, work and service contracts. The difference between the traditional and modern concessions is in the geographic extent of the concession, the time duration, and the taxation of output by value rather than the assessment of royalties on volume. For the multinational enterprise the modern concession is a more stable operating environment because it separates financial benefits from control.

Stephens, R. A. "The Risks in Business: The Political Factor." *Managing.* 3 **(1980): 13-17.**

Multinational companies are increasingly analyzing the political risks of doing business overseas. Such analysis requires a knowledge of the political climate, the government and economy of the country. Economic chaos and changes in government all contribute to risk. Corporations are either developing internal departments to cope with political risk or are hiring consultants to perform such research. Political risk assessment should be conducted in a firm or project specific manner because risk varies from sector to sector and project to project within the host country.

Stobaugh, Robert B. "How to Analyze Foreign Investment Climates." *Harvard Business Review.* **(September-October 1969): 100-8.**

Stobaugh recommends a conditional probability model for political risk assessment that is a function of the groups in power and their policy preferences vis-a-vis the multinational corporation. This political risk assessment is conducted at the micro level by individuals who are expert in the politics of the country concerned. A discount rate is developed from the joint summed probabilities of two information sets: the probability of alternative groups holding national political power and the probability of their undertaking an action that would be adverse to the local subsidiary. Scenarios can be developed on the basis of this elementary model to examine different time periods, different numbers of groups and different types and probabilities of adverse actions.

Thain, D.H. "Improving Competence to Deal with Politics and Government: The Management Challenge of the 80s." *Business Quarterly.* **45(1), (Spring 1980): 31-45.**

Thain develops a political process model to explicate the relationship between politics and government on the one hand and private business on the other. Areas covered include environmental monitoring and analysis, political risk analysis, political relationship building, strategic planning, public political action campaigns, and training and developing political leadership.

Thunell, Lars. ***Political Risks in International Business: Investment Behavior of Multinational Corporations.*** **New York: Praeger Publishers, 1977, p. 133**

Much has been made of the impact of political instability on risk and foreign investment decisionmaking. Thunell investigates the relationship between political instability in prospective host countries on investment decisions of the firm. A direct assessment of corporate investment decisionmaking was not possible. Instead, Thunell used aggregate data on investment flows collected by the Harvard Multinational Enterprise Project (establishment of new subsidiaries) and data on political instability events from the second edition of the *World Handbook of Political and Social Indicators.* Data were collected for foreign countries with at least 30 affiliates of U.S. manufacturing firms reporting to Harvard. The countries included were Mexico, Colombia, Venezuela, Brazil, Chile, Argentina, France, Italy, Spain, Nigeria, South Africa, India, Pakistan, and the Philippines.

Thunell devised seven hypotheses about the relationship of political instability to investment flows. (1) Additions to foreign investment are negatively correlated with political instability. The number of new subsidiaries should be lower in countries with higher violence scores. (2) Effects on foreign investment flows are greater for governmental instability than they are for mass political protest and violence. (3) The effect of instability on investment is negatively associated with the degree of concentration of the industry. Firms in oligopolistic industries are less influenced by political instability in the prospective host environment than are firms in more competitive industries. (4) The larger the host country market or the greater its potential for growth, the weaker will be the effect of political instability on new investment. (5) The effects of political instability are greater in labor intensive industries. (6) Among capital intensive industries, the reaction to political *instability* is greater and quicker than the reaction to political *stability*. (7) Strong ties between the home and host countries weaken the effect of political instability on investment flows.

White, Gillian. *Nationalisation of Foreign Property*. **London: Stevens and Sons, Ltd., 1961.**

Elements of international law relevant to the nationalization of foreign-owned property are discussed. Post World War II developments are presented and compared to the international legal status of foreign property prior to 1939. A discussion of the protective measures which an owner of foreign property may take when faced by nationalization is given.

Zoller, Adrien Claude. "Algerian Nationalizations: The Legal Issues." *Journal of World Trade Law*. **6 (January-February 1972): 33-57.**

Zoller reviews the legal aspects of Algeria's nationalization of foreign holdings in agriculture, small businesses, mining and oil during the early 1960s. The causes of nationalization included the coming of independence, the socialist philosophy of the new government, and the mass exodus of French owners. The Algerian government developed the following criteria for the application of nationalization law: vacant or abandoned property, unsatisfactory operation of the business, protection of law and order, and the keeping of social peace. Zoller concludes that the Algerian nationalizations were valid under international law because they were a formal act of a sovereign state, were undertaken in the public interest, were non- discriminatory, and were compensated according to traditional international legal standards.

Chapter Five: Sources of Data and Research Materials

Andrews, William G. ***International Handbook of Political Science.*** **Westport, CT: Greenwood Press, 1982, p. 464.**

Under the sponsorship of the International Political Science Association this Handbook reviews the development of political science as a discipline in 26 countries worldwide over the past half-century. Karl W. Deutsch (former IPSA President) reviews the intellectual development of political science while John Trent (IPSA Secretary General) discusses the growth of IPSA as an institution. Individual country sections, all written by national political scientists, presents information on key intellectual developments, the growth of the profession, and includes detailed information on teaching, research, professional associations and activities, and key publications. This Handbook is an indispensable guide to government officials, private sector researchers and country risk analysts who want to increase their knowledge of political science as it is practiced on an international basis.

Banks, Arthur S. ***Political Handbook of the World.*** **New York: McGraw-Hill Book Company, annual.**

This is the latest in a long series of reference works on the status of the world's major political units. Beginning in 1927 under the sponsorship of the Council on Foreign Relations, the Handbook includes country sections, regional and global overviews, and separate sections on international organizations. The country sections are the core of the

Handbook and include data on its political status, area, population, language, major urban centers, monetary system and chief of state.

Country narratives cover geography, history, government and politics, foreign relations, current issues, political parties, the legislature, the cabinet, the role of the media and international representation. Ample appendices include statistical data, membership and function of major international organizations and chronology of key international events.

Banks, Arthur S. *Economic Handbook of the World.* **New York: The Free Press, (annual).**

This companion volume to the *Political Handbook of the World* provides data and narrative discussions of the economic structure, institutions and performance of 184 countries worldwide. National participation in 88 international public and private organizations is also reviewed. Statistical data on national economic performance is supplemented by overviews of national economic institutions (trade unions, businesses, state- owned companies) and key sėctors of the economy. International transactions are also reviewed including trade, financial flows and direct investment. A chronology of international events from 1944 to the present is given.

Burtis, David; Farid Lavipour, Steven Ricciardi and Karl P. Sauvant (eds.). *Multinational Corporation–Nation–State Interaction: An Annotated Bibliography.* **New York: Prager Publishers, 1975, p.290.**

This annotated bibliography contains 714 entries published between 1964 and 1970 on the following subjects: political-economic impact of the MNC on host countries, the response of the nation-state, the response of the MNC, the response of organized labor, and the structural impact of MNCs on the international system. An item was included in the bibliography if it satisfied one of the following criteria:

(1) Provided specific hypotheses or explanations of the causes and consequences of foreign direct investment,

(2) Presented a theoretical framework for the analysis of the interaction, or,

(3) Supported or refuted hypotheses through empirical data or case studies.

Chapter II is of special interest to political risk analysts because it covers the literature on host country incentives, the business climate, guarantee programs, regulations on equity ownership, repatriation of profits and capital and personnel, expropriations, joint ventures and antitrust policy.

Curhan, Joan P., William H. Davidson, and Rajan Suri. *Tracing the Multinationals: A Sourcebook on U.S. Based Enterprises.* **Cambridge, Mass: Harvard University Press, 1977, p. 430.**

This sourcebook on U.S.-based enterprises is based on data collected by the Harvard Multinational Enterprise Project. Tables (274 in all) are presented on the following areas: proliferation of foreign subsidiaries, maturing of foreign subsidiaries, their financial statistics, employment, ownership patterns, exports and intracompany sales, and exploration and extraction activities. Two sections deal directly with political risk factors. Chapter Three, section 5 on "Expropriations" and Chapter Three, section 6 on "Methods of Exit by Period."

The Harvard Multinational Enterprise Project covers 180 U.S.-based manufacturing firms with approximately 19,000 foreign subsidiaries, and 226 foreign-based multinationals operating in manufacturing. Techniques of data collection, including the corporate questionnaire, are presented. Data are presented through 1975. Specific variables for each subsidiary include: country of operation, year of entry, method of entry, year of departure, method of departure, principal activities at entry and latest date or at departure, products manufacturered, ownership structure, sales, assets, number of employees, export sales, and intrasystem sales.

Ghertman, Michael, and James Leontiades (eds.). ***European Research in International Business.*** **Amsterdam: North Holland Publishing Company, 1978, p. 368.**

This collection of essays contains contributions on theories of international business and multinational corporations, strategic planning, ownership patterns, international finance and control, international marketing, and the international management of human resources. For the political risk analyst the article by Hans Schollhammer is of interest. Written while Schollhammer was a Fellow of the International Institute of Management, Science Center Berlin, this piece focuses on the "identification, evaluation and prediction of political risks from an international business perspective." (pp. 91-109). Schollhammer discusses the increasing significance of risk, the definition of risk and presents a political risk score based on data from the *World Handbook of Political and Social Indicators.* This risk index is based on measures of overt political violence and is used to predict government change. The relationship between political violence, government change and political risk is not argued in the piece or tested with the event- based indicators. The nexus between changes in the environment and changes in government policy towards foreign investors needs to be rigorously tested before general conclusions about the sources of risk can be made or indicator systems presented.

Gurr, Ted Robert (ed.). ***Handbook of Political Conflict: Theory and Research.*** **New York: The Free Press, 1980, p. 566.**

This Handbook is a guide to the field, an appraisal of quantitative approaches to the analysis of political violence and instability. Its outlook for the future is optimistic, if the predictions are taken as prescriptions. Gurr argues that theory and empirical work will be more closely articulated, there will be better theoretical integration across levels of analysis, that analysts will take the long-term (time- series) as well as the short-term (cross-sectional) view, and that the technology of quantitative conflict analysis will improve. Specific contributions focus on the psychological and sociological bases of conflict (Davies, Muller, Rejai); evaluations of quantitative research (Eckstein, Gurr, Zimmermann); sources of international conflict (Stohl, Zinnes, Bueno de Mesquita); outcomes of international and civil war (Stein, Russett) and the practical application of conflict research (Pirages, Nardin, Singer). The text is ably supplemented by an extensive bibliography and is indexed by author and subject.

Kurian, George Thomas. ***The Book of World Rankings.*** **New York: Facts on File Publications, 1979, p. 430.**

Kurian presents data on national economic, social, political and demographic characteristics for all countries of the world during the

1970s. Organized into 23 chapters with overview discussions and variable definitions, a total of 326 indicators are presented for the most recent datapoint available when the book went to press. Variables covered include: geography and climate, vital statistics, population and family life, race and religion, politics, foreign aid, defense spending and manpower, finance and banking, measures of national economic performance, trade, agriculture, industry and mining, labor force structure, transportation and communication, consumption patterns, health, crime, media, urbanization, and culture and sports.

Kurian, George Thomas. *Encyclopedia of the Third World.* **New York: Facts on File, 1982, 3 vols, p. 2175.**

This extensive reference on the Third World is organized into substantial country sections (12–25 pages each) and a section on general international organizations and Third World organizations that are educational, political, developmental or media oriented. Each country section includes a basic fact sheet and map, and information on geography, urbanization, topography, weather, ethno- linguistic differences, colonial experience, politics and government, current cabinet, freedom and human rights indicators, and sections on the structure and performance of the domestic and international economies. Comparative statistical tables are presented for population, GNP, foreign aid, and the activities of multinational corporations in the Third World.

Leonard, Jeffrey H. "Multinational Corporations and Politics in Developing Countries." *World Politics.* **32(3), (April 1979): 454–83.**

Leonard provides a thorough review of six major works on the role of multinational companies in the political and economic life of developing countries. These studies are Apter and Goodman, *The Multinational Corporation and Social Change*, Goodsell, *American Corporations and Peruvian Politics*, Moran, *Multinational Corporations and the Politics of Dependence*, Pinelo, *The Multinational as a Force in Latin American Politics*, Sklar, *Corporate Power in an African State*, and Tugwell, *The Politics of Oil in Venezuela*.

All six studies have a common analytic concern. How to distinguish dependence on international trade and marketing systems from dependence on the multinational corporation. Leonard reviews the debates on multinationals and economic development and the political involvement of corporations in the host country, and contrasts dependency vs. liberal approaches to the multinational corporation.

Organization for Economic Cooperation and Development. *Stock of Private Direct Investments by Development Assistance Committee Countries in Developing Countries, End 1967.* **Paris: OECD, 1972, p. 170.**

This standard reference work presents data on the stock of foreign investment in developing countries. The data are disaggregated by investing country, sector and country of incorporation. The capital-exporting states that are members of the Development Assistance Committee are: Australia, Austria, Belgium, Canada, Denmark, France, West Germany, Italy, Japan, the Netherlands, Norway, Portugal, Sweden, Switzerland, the U.K., and the U.S. Economic sectors are disaggregated as follows: petroleum, mining and smelting, agriculture, manufacturing, trade, public utilities, transportation, banking, tourism and a residual category.

Organization for Economic Cooperation and Development. *Investing in Developing Countries.* **Paris: OECD, 1978, p. 121.**

This manual reviews the insurance and investment guaranty programs of OECD members of the Development Assistance Committee. Multilateral investment protection schemes are discussed as are exchange controls and other restrictions on the movement of capital. Tables on private investment flows and stocks are presented.

Organization for Economic Cooperation and Development. *International Investment and Multinational Enterprises: Recent International Direct Investment Trends, 1981.* **Paris, OECD, 1981, p. 106.**

The focus of this report is on the sending rather than the receiving countries. The volume and direction of direct investment flows from Australia, Belgium, Canada, France, West Germany, Japan, the Netherlands, Sweden, the U.K. and the U.S. for all industries are presented. Recent slow growth overall masks important differences. One development is the increase in West European and Japanese direct investment in the U.S. Another is the growth of investments in services rather than manufacturing or resource extraction. The data are presented in detailed country matrices covering investment flows by year and sector from 1966 through 1979.

Ryans, Cynthia C. *International Business Reference Sources.* **Lexington, MA: Lexington Books, 1983, p. 195.**

This annotated bibliography is oriented to both the practitioner and student of international business. In four chapters, it presents information on government publications, subscriptions, and continuations, international business data sources, and international business books (marketing, finance, economics). A substantial appendix presents names and addresses of national and international organizations from which country and product data may be obtained.

Entries are indexed by title and author. Each entry contains a full bibliographic reference, Library of Congress call number, price and ordering information and, generally, a short, descriptive annotation.

Sanders, David. *Patterns of Political Instability.* **New York: St. Martin's Press, 1981, p. 244.**

Sanders provides an overview of political instability. Instability is defined, its dimensions are characterized, the major analytic approaches are critiqued and inconsistencies between the findings of empirical/quantitative analyses are documented. Four predictive models of political instability are developed and tested with national level, time-series data on political protest violence, governmental change and measures of national economic, social and political attributes. Peaceful change, violent protest, government change and political regime change (revolution) are modelled with data drawn from the second edition of the *World Handbook of Political and Social Indicators.*

Peaceful instability is explained least well (R–square of 22 percent). Violent change is explained moderately well (48 percent) as is government change (46 percent). The most tumultuous form of political instability – revolution – is explained best (53 percent). However, these models explain at best half of the cross-country variation in political instability, leaving much to be resolved without the use of quantitative techniques.

Factors consistently shown to be important in causing political violence are socioeconomic change, ethno-linguistic fractionalization, trade dependency, the level and rate of change of development and the ability/willingness of governments to suppress dissent. Communist regimes during the period 1948–67 demonstrated high coercive capacity and, hence, a high level of regime stability.

Singer, J. David, and Michael D. Wallace (eds.). *To Augur Well: Early Warning Indicators in World Politics.* **Beverly Hills: Sage Publications, 1979, p. 308.**

This edited collection examines sources of conflict in national and international politics and presents tools for modelling and predicting such conflict. Approaches are derived at the level of the international system which focus on the distribution of national capability and status, alliance structures, status inconsistencies, and geographic proximity. National properties that are relevant to both internal and external conflict include population growth, economic performance, government institutional capacity, and societal unrest.

Gurr and Lichbach present an econometric forecasting model of the intensity and extent of two forms of domestic political instability: protest and rebellion. Political instability is defined by Gurr and Lichbach as activity directed against the governing regime or the political system. Protest is composed of peaceful and violent events that are relatively spontaneous: demonstrations, strikes and riots. Rebellion is composed of violent, organized events that are directed at the structure of the political system: armed attacks, terrorism, and assassinations. Forecasting models are developed and applied to a wide range of developing countries with data from the 1960s and 1970s.

Sivard, Ruth Leger. *World Military and Social Expenditures.* **Leesburg, Virginia: WMSE Publications, annual.**

WMSE publications document military spending, research and development and arms transfers on a worldwide basis. Social indicators are also included measuring GNP per capita and health/educational expenditures. The statistical annexes, while two to three years behind, present several years of data for 140 countries on population, urbanization, land area, population density, GNP,military spending, participation in international peacekeeping, expenditures for education, health and foreign economic assistance, military manpower, the number of physicians and teachers and measures of educational, health and nutritional attainments. These data are are also available on computer tape through the Inter-University Consortium for Political and Social Research, Ann Arbor, Michigan.

Taylor, Charles Lewis (ed.). *Indicator Systems for Political, Economic and Social Analysis.* **Cambridge, Mass: Oelgeschlager, Gunn and Hain, 1980, p. 242.**

This edited collection is based on an international conference held at the Science Center Berlin during the summer of 1978. The contributors focused on the development of indicator systems for measuring economic growth, government performance, social welfare and political stability. Papers are presented on the data collection programs of the International Labor Organization, UNESCO and the UN (demographic data). Measurement issues, rather than substantive conclusions, are the central concerns of this study.

Taylor, Charles Lewis and David A. Jodice. *World Handbook of Political and Social Indicators, III. Volume I: Cross- National*

Attributes and Rates of Change. **New Haven: Yale University Press, 1983, p. 305.**

Data on the following types of indicators are presented for 155 countries at five year intervals beginning in 1950: size of government and allocation of public resources; total and sectoral expenditure and revenue of the central government; distribution of GNP by government consumption, private consumption and investment; measures of political and civil rights; political and economic discrimination; political separatism; organization of labor; voter turnout; party fractionalization; energy production and consumption; GNP, GNP per capita; land area; vital statistics; nutrition; health care; social mobility and economic structure. Data on levels and rates of change are presented. Most recent data are for 1978.

Taylor, Charles Lewis and David A. Jodice. *World Handbook of Political and Social Indicators III: Volume 2: Political Protest and Government Change.* **New Haven: Yale University Press, 1983, p. 216.**

Political event data are presented for 136 countries for the period 1948–77. Coverage is worldwide. Events were coded from reports in the elite press *(eg. New York Times)* and compendia of local news sources. Approximately twenty-five different types of events are coded. Data are presented at the daily, quarterly and annual level. Descriptive information (actor, duration, effects, purpose, etc.) is coded for each event of political protest.

Taylor, Charles Lewis and David A. Jodice. *The Third World Handbook of Political and Social Indicators: Codebook.* **Cologne:**

Zentralarchiv fur Empirische Sozialforschung, November 1982, p. 284.

This codebook documents the aggregate and political event data from the two volumes of the third edition of the *World Handbook of Political and Social Indicators.* Data tapes are available from the Zentralarchiv or the Inter-University Consortium for Political and Social Research, Ann Arbor, Michigan.

U.S. Department of Commerce. *U.S. Direct Investment Abroad, 1966: Final Data.* **Washington, D.C: U.S. Government Printing Office, 1974, p. 289.**

This volume contains the final data derived from the 1966 benchmark survey of U.S. foreign direct investment. Under the reporting requirements of the Bretton Woods Agreement Act, the Commerce Department mailed questionnaires to 3,400 U.S. firms owning approximately 23,000 affiliates worldwide.

Over 200 tables are presented, disaggregated by country of operation and industry. Types of data collected include: value of U.S. direct investment position abroad, balance of payments transactions related to U.S. direct foreign investment, foreign affiliate financial and operating data, and number of U.S. owned foreign affiliates by country of operation and industry.

Except in cases where disclosure would compromise a reporting firm's confidentiality, data on each series are provided for the following 53 countries of operation: Canada, United Kingdom, Belgium, Luxembourg, France, West Germany, Italy, the Netherlands, Denmark, Ireland, Norway, Spain, Sweden, Switzerland, Austria, Greece, Portugal,

Turkey, Japan, Australia, New Zealand, South Africa, Argentina, Brazil, Chile, Colombia, Mexico, Panama, Peru, Venezuela, Costa Rica, El Salvador, Guatemala, Honduras, Nicaragua, Bahamas, Bermuda, Jamaica, Liberia, Libya, Nigeria, Iran, Israel, India, Indonesia, Philippines, Hong Kong, South Korea, Malaysia, Pakistan, Singapore, Taiwan, and Thailand.

U.S. Department of Commerce. *Investment Climates in Foreign Countries.* **Washington, D.C: U.S. Government Printing Office, 1983, p. 1270.**

This four volume study was prepared in 1982 from reports of U.S. embassies based on generally-available sources. Volume I includes OECD countries and other European countries. Volume II covers Africa. Volume III covers Asia (except Japan which is covered in Volume I). Volume IV covers the Western Hemisphere (except Canada which is in Volume I).

These investment climate statements summarize the laws, policies, and economic climates of host countries which may affect U.S. direct investments. Specific topics include infrastructure development, labor supply, host government policies in the areas of taxation, nationalization, anti-trust, foreign exchange, repatriation of capital and earnings, investment incentives and performance requirements. Existing foreign investment disputes are described and expectations about changes in host country investment policies are presented.

U.S. Department of Commerce. *U.S. Business Investments in Foreign Countries, 1960.* **Washington, D.C: U.S. Government Printing Office, 1960.**

This study presents benchmark data on the overseas investments and operations of affiliates with at least 10 percent U.S. ownership. Extensive tables present data on direct investment by country, year and sector. Data cover the years 1929, 1946, 1950, 1957, and 1959. The narrative provides an overview of investment and operations by regions and industries, and data on extent of assets and financial structure, sales and expenses of foreign subsidiaries, earnings and remittances, capital flows from the U.S., sources and uses of funds at the subsidiary level, and balance of payments effects. In countries were few American firms are operating, data are aggregated or withheld to protect the confidentiality of firms responding to the Commerce Department's survey.

U.S. Department of Commerce. ***Selected Data on U.S. Direct Investment Abroad, 1966–76.*** **Washington, D.C: U.S. Government Printing Office, 1977, p. 90.**

Data for eleven years are presented by country and industry for the following indicators: U.S. direct investment position at year end; net capital outflows, reinvested earnings, earnings, fees and royalties, and license fees.

U.S. Department of Commerce. ***U.S. Direct Investment Abroad, 1977.*** **Washington, D.C: U.S. Government Printing Office, 1981, p. 516.**

The Bureau of Economic Analysis commissioned another benchmark study to measure the investments and operations of U.S. firms abroad. Reporting was compulsory for U.S. companies with at least a 10 percent ownership in foreign subsidiaries. A total of 3,540 U.S. firms replied with data on 24,666 foreign affiliates. 11,123 other foreign affiliates were listed as exempt from the Commerce Department's survey but they account for a very small proportion of total direct investment. Again, data points are suppressed if disclosure would lead to the identification of specific U.S. companies or individuals operating abroad.

Specific indicators include financing of foreign affiliates, balance of payments transactions, direct investment position, capital outflows, investment income and direct investment fees and royalties.

United Nations, Centre on Transnational Corporations. *Nationalization or Takeover of Foreign Enterprises: A Select Bibliography.* **New York: United Nations, 1974, p. 17.**

Concern at the United Nations about permanent sovereignty over natural resources prompted the presentation of this 200 item bibliography on nationalization. The materials cover the post-1960 period only and were listing only if they were available in the Dag Hammarskjold Library. No annotations are presented.

U. S. Department of Commerce. *U.S. Direct Investment Abroad, 1966. Part I: Balance of Payments Data.* **Washington, D.C: U.S. Government Printing Office, 1971, p. 239.**

This benchmark study reports data on foreign investment trends and operations of 23,000 affiliates of 3,400 reporting parent U.S. owned companies. Data series include capital flows, net earnings, income receipts, reinvestment of earnings, payments of royalties and fees, and number of affiliates. Data are disaggregated by industry, type of transaction and country or region of incorporation.

Country specific data are reported for Argentina, Brazil, Chile, Colombia, Mexico, Panama, Peru, Uruguay, Venezuela, Bahamas, Bermuda, Jamaica, Trinidad and Tobago, Belgium, France, West Germany, Italy, Luxembourg, the Netherlands, Austria, Denmark, Finland, Ireland, Norway, Portugal, Spain, Sweden, Switzerland, Turkey, the United Kingdom, Canada, Algeria, Egypt, Liberia, Nigeria, Rhodesia, (now Zimbabwe), South Africa, Iran, Israel, Australia, Hong Kong, India, Japan, New Zealand, the Philippines, and Tawain.

U. S. Department of Commerce. *U.S. Direct Investment Abroad, 1966. Part II: Investment Position, Financial and Operating Data.* **Washington, D.C: U.S. Government Printing Office, 1971.**

This second part of the 1966 benchmark study reports on the financial position, operations, and sales of approximately 23,000 affiliates of 3,400 reporting firms. Firms cover all sectors of the economy (petroleum, mining, manufacturing, utilities, transportation, communication, finance, retail trade) for all U.S. direct investors with a minimum 10 percent interest in a foreign affiliate. Data points are suppressed if their disclosure would reveal company-specific information.

U.S. Department of State. *Terrorist Attacks Against Diplomats* **Washington, D.C: Bureau of Public Affairs, December 1981, p. 16.**

This report provides a statistical overview of international terrorist attacks on diplomatic personnel and facilities from January 1968 to June 1981. Attacks against diplomats have become more frequent and widespread. In 1970, there were 213 attacks against diplomats from 31 countries. In 1980 there were 409 attacks against diplomats from 60 countries. The pattern of terrorist events is described by year of the event, country, direct target, and casualties. Substantial appendices include lists of countries whose diplomats have been victimized by international terrorism, a list of countries where such events have occured and a list of terrorist groups and common acronyms.

U.S. Department of State. *Patterns of International Terrorism: 1981.* **Washington, D.C.; Office for Combatting Terrorism, July 1982, p. 21.**

This annual publication catalogues the number, type, and effects of international terrorism in the most recent year. Terrorism and international terrorism are defined. Comparisons are made back to January 1, 1968 when the collection of data began. Since 1968, 7,425 incidents have taken place resulting in 8,088 victims being held hostage and 12,139 deaths or injuries. The activities of specific groups are discussed in detail: Provisional Irish Republican Army, Red Army Faction, Red Brigades, Basque Fatherland and Liberty. Western Europe has been the location of a plurality of terrorist actions. This is due to the activity of the groups listed above and the use of major capitals like London and Paris as battlegrounds by Middle Eastern terrorists.

U.S. Department of State. *Terrorist Attacks Against U.S. Business.* **Washington, D.C: Office for Combatting Terrorism, June 1982, p. 20.**

A significant, if episodic, source of political risk are actions directed against U.S. businessmen by international terrorists or even political factions that are wholly local in character. The 1984 slaying of two Chevron employees in the Sudan is a grim reminder of the vulnerability of U.S. personnel and, by extension, facilities overseas. The Department of State prepares annual studies documenting the number, location, types, and casualties in these events. The groups responsible for such acts, where known, are also presented. Data have been collected beginning January 1, 1968. Wherever possible, time-series data are presented. Types of incidents include kidnappings, hostage-takings, bombings, armed attacks, hijackings, assassination, and sabotage. Through June 1982, there have been 953 international terrorist events directed against 128 firms. Attacks against U.S. businessmen (intentionally or accidentally) account for one-third of all terrorist acts directed against Americans.

U.S. Department of State, Bureau of Intelligence and Research. *Nationalization, Expropriation and Other Takings of U.S. and Certain Foreign Property Since 1960.* **Washington, D.C: Department of State, 1971;** *Disputes Involving U.S. Foreign Direct Investment: July 1, 1971 through July 31, 1973; Disputes Involving U.S. Foreign Direct Investment: August 31, 1973 through January 1, 1975; Disputes Involving U.S. Foreign Direct Investment: February 1, 1975 through February 28, 1977.* **Washington, D.C: Department of State, serial.**

These State Department publications provide a listing of disputes between host governments and U.S. firms. The listing is by country and the status (continuing, resolved) of the action. These reports describe the trends in disputes over time and examine causes of economic nationalism in the developing countries. These causes are, broadly, political expediency, assertion of local control, a desire to reverse dependent relationships and the increasing technical competence of the host countries themselves.

Vaupel, James C., and Joan P. Curhan. *The World's Multinational Enterprises.* **Boston: Harvard University Press, 1973, p. 505.**

This volume reports a portion of the data collected by the Harvard Multinational Enterprise Project on the foreign activities of large U.S. and selected non-U.S. multinational enterprises. Data for affiliates of U.S. firms cover from 1900 to 1968 and for foreign firms from 1900 to 1971. Firms were selected from *Fortune's* listings of the 500 largest U.S. industrial corporations and the 500 largest non-U.S. industrial corporations. Twenty-nine variables are reported for each affiliate. These variables include: date of entry and termination in the host country, country code, region code, 1970 GNP and 1970 GNP per capita in country of incorporation, principle industry, equity ownership structure, parent firm nationality, value of sales, research and development expenditures of the parent firm, and the geographic spread of the activities of the parent system.

Wallace, Don (ed.). ***International Regulation of the Multinational Corporation.*** **New York: Praeger Publishers, 1976, p. 235.**

Multinational corporations are defined and the scope of their increasing activities is described. The activities of the multinational that are subject to regulation are listed. Existing proposals (UN, OECD) to regulate these companies on an international basis are presented. Given that the nation-state is the manager of the national political economy, certain issues will be beyond the pale for an international investment agency. These include local control over general social, economic and tax legislation, joint venture policy and incentives, economic planning, national programs of investment insurance and labor legislation. Wallace's proposal for an international investment agency is based on the principle of an open world economy, traditional standards of international law, progressive liberalization of national barriers to trade and investment, non-discrimination, and safeguards to minimize jurisdictional overlap.

Wilkins, Mira. *The Maturing of Multinational Enterprise: American Business Abroad from 1914 to 1970.* **Cambridge, Mass: Harvard University Press, 1974, p. 590.**

This is a narrative history of the expansion of American enterprise abroad based on data collected by the Harvard Multinational Enterprise Project. There are three major themes in this reference work. The first is the dramatic challenge posed by American business to European interests throughout the 1914–70 period. The second is the variety of responses by host governments in both the developed and developing areas to multinational enterprises. The third major theme is the cumulative change in international economic relations brought about American businesses abroad. The four major epochs in the history of American business abroad are (1) pre-World War I and tentative beginnings; (2) the prosperous twenties and the increasing commitment of U.S. companies to overseas activities; (3) the cautious 1930s; and, (4) a veritable explosion after 1945.

World Bank. *World Bank Atlas.* **Washington, D.C: World Bank, (annual).**

The *World Bank Atlas* is a handy reference aid to the countries of the world and their current economic situation. Descriptions of the data and broad international trends are provided in English, French and Spanish. Data are organized by national income level for 185 countries worldwide. Specific data items are GNP, GNP per capita, population and rates of growth in GNP over several intervals. Data are generally only one year out of date.

World Bank. *World Development Report.* **Washington, D.C: World Bank, (annual).**

The *World Development Report* contains a narrative on several aspects of development as well as statistical tables on the economic performance of developing countries. The narrative sections focus on prospects for development, international policy issues such as LDC debt and capital flows, employment, population planning, industrialization and urbanization. Prospects for primary producers and semi-industrial states are compared. Data from the vast holdings of the World Bank are reprinted in this annual. Specific indicators include: population, inflation, area, GNP, GNP per capita, adult literacy, life expectancy, GDP growth, sectoral distribution of GDP, change in major demand aggregates (public and private consumption, gross investment), merchandise trade (levels and change in structure), balance of payments, debt-service ratios and international capital flows.

World Bank. *World Tables 1980.* Washington, D.C: World Bank, 1980, p. 474.

This reference work reports selected data from the World Bank's holdings on the economic, social and international financial condition of most developing and developed market economies. The focus of the collection is on the developing countries. The data are presented in three sections. Economic Data Sheet I contains information on population growth, national accounts and prices. Data are presented for 1950, 1955, 1960 and are annual from 1965 to 1977. Economic Data Sheet II contains 58 series on balance of payments, external public debt, foreign trade indexes and central government finances. Data are presented in U.S. and local currencies or as indexes. Economic Data Sheet III contains comparative economic, social and international data. These series are presented to facilitate comparisons between countries at different levels of development.

World Future Society. *The Future: A Guide to Information Resources.* **Washington, D.C: World Future Society, 1979, p. 722.**

This is a directory of organizations, individuals and research projects concerned with analyzing the future. For each organization the following data are reported: address, constituent organizations, staff, budget, source of support, objectives, major programs, special facilities and publications. The directory also lists publications, reports and books of interest to students of the the future. Educational course, firms, audiotapes and games and simulations are also listed. Geographic and subject indexes are also provided.

Zimmermann, Ekkart. *Political Violence, Crises and Revolution: Theories and Research.* **Cambridge, Mass: Schenkman Publishing Company, 1983, p. 792.**

This is a first class reference work on comparative empirical analyses of revolution and theoretical work about a wide variety of political changes. In an extensive overview of the literature complemented by a 240 page bibliography. Zimmermann reviews major approaches to four varieties of instability (political violence, crises, coups, revolutions) by presenting the theoretical basis of the approach, data that have been collected in accordance with the theory, methods of analysis and substantive findings.

Index

ABOUT THE COMPILER

David A. Jodice is currently Director of Survey Research at Polimetrics, Inc., a Maryland-based consulting firm. Dr. Jodice has taught at Harvard and Georgetown Universities and is the author of numerous scholarly articles. He has recently published, with Charles L. Taylor, the third edition of the *World Handbook of Political and Social Indicators.*